THE SPACE RACE

THE SPACE RACE

THE THRILLING HISTORY OF NASA'S RACE TO THE MOON, FROM PROJECT MERCURY TO APOLLO 11 AND BEYOND

JOHN C. HAMILTON

RavenFire
Media, Inc.

RavenFire Media, Inc.

The Space Race Copyright © 2019 by John C. Hamilton.

Last updated July 2022.

All Rights Reserved.

No part of this book may be reproduced in any form or by any electronic or mechanical means, including information storage and retrieval systems, without written permission from the author, except for the use of brief quotations in a book review.

Photos courtesy NASA.

Front cover: Apollo 16 astronaut John Young salutes as he leaps above the lunar surface, April 1972.

Back cover: Apollo 17 astronaut Harrison "Jack" Schmitt goes for a moonwalk, December 1972.

ISBN: 978-0-9828459-6-7

www.johnchamilton.com

CONTENTS

MISSILES AND SPY SATELLITES

1. The Space Race — 3
2. Early Rockets — 5
3. How Rockets Work — 7
4. Rocket Pioneers — 9
5. The V-2 Missile — 11
6. Wernher von Braun — 15
7. Sergei Korolev — 18
8. The Cold War — 20
9. The ICBM — 21
10. Sputnik — 23
11. America's Turn — 26
12. High-Flying Spies — 28

PROJECT MERCURY

13. Project Mercury — 33
14. The Mercury 7 — 35
15. The Mercury Spacecraft — 37
16. Animals in Space — 39
17. Yuri Gagarin — 41
18. Freedom 7 — 43
19. Kennedy's Challenge — 46
20. Liberty Bell 7 — 48
21. Friendship 7 — 51
22. Mercury Spacesuits — 56
23. Aurora 7 — 58
24. Human Computers — 60
25. Sigma 7 — 62
26. Faith 7 — 64

PROJECT GEMINI

27. Project Gemini	69
28. The Space Race Heats Up	71
29. The Gemini Spacecraft	73
30. Gemini 3	75
31. Gemini 4	78
32. Gemini 5	82
33. Rendezvous: Gemini 6A and 7	84
34. Gemini 8	87
35. Gemini 9A	91
36. Gemini 10	94
37. Gemini 11	96
38. Gemini 12	98

PROJECT APOLLO

39. The First Footsteps on the Moon	103
40. Moon Probes	105
41. Monster Rockets	107
42. The Apollo Spacecraft	109
43. A Trip to the Moon	111
44. Apollo 1 Tragedy	112
45. Soyez 1	114
46. Apollo 7	116
47. Apollo 8	118
48. Apollo 9	121
49. Apollo 10	123
50. Apollo 11	124
51. Apollo 12	129
52. Apollo 13	131
53. Apollo 14	135
54. Apollo 15	137
55. Apollo 16	140
56. Apollo 17	142

SPACE STATIONS AND BEYOND

57. Beyond the Space Race	147
58. Salyut Space Stations	150
59. Soyuz Spacecraft	152

60. Soyuz 11 Tragedy	154
61. Skylab	156
62. Apollo-Soyuz Test Project	159
63. Space Shuttle	161
64. The Challenger and Columbia Tragedies	164
65. Mir Space Station	166
66. International Space Station	168
67. Future Space Stations	173

ASTRONAUTS AND COSMONAUTS

68. Buzz Aldrin	179
69. Neil Armstrong	181
70. Guy Bluford	184
71. Frank Borman	185
72. Scott Carpenter	186
73. Gene Cernan	187
74. Leroy Chiao	188
75. Michael Collins	189
76. Pete Conrad	191
77. Gordon Cooper	192
78. Yuri Gagarin	193
79. John Glenn	194
80. Gus Grissom	196
81. Chris Hadfield	198
82. Scott Kelly	199
83. Alexey Leonov	201
84. Jim Lovell	202
85. Sally Ride	204
86. Wally Schirra	205
87. David Scott	206
88. Alan Shepard	207
89. Deke Slayton	209
90. Velentina Tereshkova	210
91. Gherman Titov	211
92. Ed White	212
93. Peggy Whitson	213
94. John Young	215

Also in the Destination Outer Space Series	219
Get a Free Book	221
Please Leave a Review	223
Timeline	225
Glossary	233
Selected Bibliography	239
About the Author	245
Also by John C. Hamilton	247

"We choose to go to the Moon in this decade and do the other things, not because they are easy, but because they are hard; because that goal will serve to organize and measure the best of our energies and skills, because that challenge is one that we are willing to accept, one we are unwilling to postpone, and one we intend to win… ."

PRESIDENT JOHN F. KENNEDY

MISSILES AND SPY SATELLITES

CHAPTER 1
THE SPACE RACE

After World War II ended in 1945, two superpowers emerged: the United States and the Soviet Union. These two allies combined forces during the war to defeat the worldwide threat of Nazi Germany, Japan, and Italy. After the war, however, their partnership quickly fell apart.

Each side wanted to show the world that its system of government was best. The conquest of space was a perfect way to show off their superior technology. At first, the military drove the space race. Each side worked to build better rockets and missiles that could strike targets across the oceans. Spy satellites were sent into orbit so suspicious generals and politicians could keep an eye on the enemy.

With time, another goal arose. Both the United States and the Soviet Union vowed to put people into space. The ultimate goal: to land someone on the Moon.

Apollo 11 launches on July 16, 1969. Astronauts Neil Armstrong, Buzz Aldrin, and Michael Collins sit atop the powerful Saturn V rocket, heading toward the Moon.

CHAPTER 2
EARLY ROCKETS

MODERN ROCKETS ARE POWERFUL ENOUGH TO SEND SPACECRAFT billions of miles beyond the edge of our Solar System. The history of the Space Race, however, began hundreds of years ago, when rockets were simple toys.

Around 400 BC, a Greek man named Archytas lived in the southern city of Tarentum, Italy. He amused people by making a wooden pigeon "fly." Archytas partly filled the wooden bird with water and then heated it over a fire. The water turned to steam and shot out of a hole in the pigeon. The toy was then thrust in the opposite direction.

Three hundred years after Archytas, a Greek named Hero, from the city of Alexandria, invented another steam-powered curiosity. He mounted a sphere above a kettle of water. A fire under the kettle turned the water to steam. The steam forcefully escaped through two L-shaped tubes. This caused the sphere to rotate rapidly, to the amazement of everyone who saw it.

Nobody really knows when or where true rockets were invented. It probably happened somewhere in China during the first century AD. Chinese chemists experimented with early forms of gunpowder and used it to make fireworks. They made fireworks by putting the explosives in bamboo tubes. When set on fire, the escaping gasses from the gunpowder caused the tubes to fly through the air. The Chinese also attached the bamboo tubes to arrows. These solid-fuel "fire arrows" flew straighter than the bamboo rockets alone.

The first known use of rockets in warfare happened in 1232 at the Battle of Kai-Ken. The Chinese used masses of fire arrows to kill and frighten invaders from Mongolia.

CHAPTER 3
HOW ROCKETS WORK

THINK OF A ROCKET AS IF IT WERE A BALLOON. FIRST, YOU INFLATE IT with air. When you squeeze shut the neck, or nozzle, there is a pressure inside the balloon that is greater than the air outside. The balloon stays where it is because the air presses equally against the inside walls. The pressure is the same in every direction.

When you let go of the nozzle, you create an imbalance in the balloon. The internal pressure at the front of the balloon is now greater than the pressure at the back. The air shoots out of the hole, and the balloon is thrust forward. This shows physicist Sir Isaac Newton's third law of motion: for every action in nature, there is an equal and opposite reaction.

A balloon shows how rocket propulsion works. However, with balloons, the pressurized gas is the air trapped inside. With rockets, the pressurized gas is produced by burning propellants. These may be solid, liquid, or some of each.

Modern rockets use the same basic science as the balloon example. One big difference is that rockets get their thrust by burning fuel, such as liquid hydrogen. In order to burn something, you need oxygen. Normal jet engines get their oxygen from the air they fly through. Rockets can work in the vacuum of space because they carry their own oxygen (an oxidizer), such as supercooled liquid oxygen. The fuel and oxidizer are mixed together and burned in a combustion chamber at the back of the rocket. The hot, pressurized gas spews out of the engine. Following Newton's third law of motion, the rocket then moves forward in the opposite direction.

CHAPTER 4
ROCKET PIONEERS

In 1865, French novelist Jules Verne (1801-1899) published the science fiction classic *From the Earth to the Moon*. Three adventurers climb inside a spacecraft shaped like a bullet and are shot out of an enormous cannon toward the Moon. Their story of exploration fired the public's imagination. Many wondered if rockets could really someday take astronauts into space.

One of those dreamers was a Russian schoolteacher named Konstantin Tsiolkovsky (1857-1935). He was a self-taught physicist and mathematician. In 1903, he published a scientific paper called *The Exploration of Cosmic Space by Means of Reaction Devices*. At a time when cars and airplanes had just been invented, Tsiolkovsky (Sil-kof-skee) correctly showed how rockets could be used to travel in space. He also described multistage rockets, air locks, and rockets propelled by liquid oxygen and hydrogen. Many of his ideas are used in spacecraft today.

Another early rocket scientist was Romanian-born Hermann Oberth (1894-1989). In 1923, he published *The Rocket into Planetary Space*. He moved to Germany at age 18 and lived there for the rest of his life. His work demonstrated how powerful, multistage rockets could escape Earth's gravity.

Along with Tsiolkovsky and Oberth, American physicist

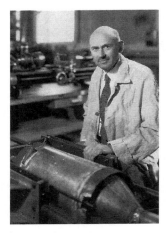

Robert Goddard

Robert Goddard (1882-1945) is known today as one of the three fathers of modern rocketry. In 1926, he became the first person to successfully build and test a rocket using liquid fuel. He proved rockets can work in the airless vacuum of space. He also invented ways to steer rockets in flight and made pumps for rocket fuel. In honor of his pioneering work, NASA named Maryland's Goddard Space Flight Center after him.

CHAPTER 5
THE V-2 MISSILE

By the 1930s, many nations realized rockets could be powerful weapons. Scientists worked to invent long-range missiles that could carry explosives and fly automatically.

One of the most terrifying weapons of World War II (1939-1945) was the German V-2 missile. First flown by the Nazis in 1942, the V-2 carried 2,000 pounds (907 kg) of explosives at targets about 200 miles (322 km) away. Using a potent mix of ethyl alcohol and liquid oxygen fuel, the V-2 became the first man-made object to reach space.

After launch, the 46-foot (14-m) -tall missile was guided to its target by gyroscopes and rudders. The V-2 was a ballistic missile. In other words, it was a gravity bomb. Once its fuel supply was cut off, it simply fell back to Earth, like a baseball that is hit into left field.

During World War II, the German military recruited a team of scientists to develop the V-2 missile. They were led by aerospace engineer Wernher von Braun (1912-1977). The missile was officially called the A-4, although it was widely known as the V-2. The "V" stood for a German word that means "vengeance weapon."

Von Braun and his team built and tested V-2 missiles on a

German military base at Peenemünde, on the coast of the Baltic Sea. British bomber attacks forced the Germans to move farther inland. A secret underground factory called Mittelwerk was built near the town of Nordhausen. Slave workers from the Mittelbau-Dora concentration camp were used to make over 5,000 V-2s. The conditions in the tunnels were very harsh. Approximately 20,000 overworked prisoners died.

Germany began launching large numbers of V-2s in late 1944. Between September 1944 and March 1945, more than 2,900 missiles were fired at targets in England, France, and Belgium. The V-2 could cross the English Channel and strike London, England, in less than five minutes. On December 16, 1944, a V-2 struck the Rex Cinema in Antwerp, Belgium, killing 567 people and injuring 194. Eleven buildings were destroyed. It was the single deadliest V-2 attack of the war.

THE V-2 MISSILE

The V-2 was used as a weapon of terror. It flew so high and fast that there was no warning, and no way to shoot it down (unlike the earlier, slower German V-1 "buzz bomb" missile). When it struck the ground, its payload of explosives ignited, strong enough to devastate an entire city block.

Even though the V-2 was destructive, the missile program overall was unsuccessful. About 7,000 people were killed by V-2s in Europe, but many more thousands died making them. The V-2's primitive guidance system often caused it to miss its target and explode harmlessly in the countryside. Also, each V-2 was extremely expensive to make, about the same as a fighter airplane. But unlike an airplane, the V-2 did limited damage (if it hit a target at all) and could only be used once.

Despite these problems, the V-2 was a breakthrough in missile design. Its guidance system was an important new technology that other countries wanted.

As the war came to an end in 1945, the V-2's lead scientist, Wernher von Braun, had a decision to make. He knew that the Americans, the British, and the Soviets wanted the plans to the V-2. Which side would he surrender to?

WHAT IS THE DIFFERENCE BETWEEN A ROCKET AND A MISSILE?

A very simple explanation is that rockets go straight in the direction they are pointed. Missiles are guided, usually by a computer or a sensor that steers it toward a distant target.

German V-2s had rocket engines that made the craft fly upwards. Gyroscopes and simple steering vanes kept them on course, making them early ground-to-ground missiles. Today, missiles can can stay on course by detecting heat or other kinds of energy. They can also be guided by lasers or satellites.

In simple military terms, a missile usually has a warhead that contains explosives, chemicals, or biological weapons. Rockets, on the other hand, usually carry scientific instruments, or even astronauts. However, some rockets are guided, like missiles. It is confusing, and the two terms are often used interchangeably.

CHAPTER 6
WERNHER VON BRAUN

When Wernher von Braun (1912-1977) was a child growing up in Germany, his mother gave him a telescope. This made him excited to learn about astronomy. His imagination was also fired by the science fiction books of authors Jules Verne and H.G. Wells.

| Wernher von Braun.

As a young man, von Braun was influenced by the work of rocket scientist Hermann Oberth. Von Braun learned math and physics to better understand rocketry. He also joined a German rocket club called the Society for Space Travel.

The work of von Braun and his team of scientists came to the attention of the German military. In 1932, they went to work developing weapons for Adolf Hitler and the Nazis. It was a way for von Braun to invent different rocket designs.

Wernher von Braun was officially a Nazi, but he was more interested in space exploration. He wanted the primary goal of the V-2 program to be manned spaceflight. As World War II dragged on, however, von Braun realized his missiles would only be used by the Germans as weapons of war.

Von Braun is a controversial figure today. He surely knew that slave labor was being used to construct V-2 missiles. But by the time he was aware of these war crimes, could he do anything about it? Maybe he could have secretly sabotaged the missile program, or even fled Germany. However, von Braun was too blinded by his dream of spaceflight. He needed the German military to continue his research, and so he did nothing.

By 1945, the Germans had suffered many battlefield defeats. The war seemed lost. Von Braun knew that American and Soviet military forces were racing to capture V-2 rockets and plans. The Soviets had captured the German Peenemünde rocket launch site in the spring. Now they wanted to snatch the brains behind the missiles.

With American and Soviet forces driving deeper into Germany, von Braun and his team were shuttled from town to town. Their guards were ordered to execute them rather than allow them to be captured. As the war finally neared its end, the guards let many of the scientists roam freely.

In May 1945, von Braun surrendered to the American Army. It was his best chance to continue his rocket research. He also didn't want V-2 technology to fall into the hands of the Soviet government, which was run by the brutal dictator Joseph Stalin.

The US Army had a plan called Operation Paperclip. It secretly sent German rocket scientists and V-2 parts back to America. Von Braun and about 125 members of his rocketry team worked for the Army at Fort Bliss, Texas. They designed new rockets and also helped teach American scientists how to assemble and launch captured V-2s at the nearby White Sands Proving Ground (later called the White Sands Missile Range) in New Mexico. They later worked at the Army's Redstone Arsenal near Huntsville, Alabama, and were eventually transferred to NASA's Marshall Space Flight Center. Von Braun became the center's first director.

During his long career, Wernher von Braun and his team helped design many rockets and missiles. They included the Redstone rocket, the Jupiter missile, the Pershing missile, as well as the Saturn rockets that took American astronauts to the Moon.

CHAPTER 7
SERGEI KOROLEV

NEAR THE END OF WORLD WAR II, IN 1945, AS THE SOVIET RED Army swept through eastern Germany, it captured every rocket scientist it could find. The Soviets were eager to learn their secrets. The big prize, however, was top German rocket designer Wernher von Braun and his team of engineers. But they had already been snatched up by the Americans. The Soviets would have to find someone else to help them build better rockets.

As a young man growing up in the 1910s and 1920s, Sergei Korolev (1906-1966) fell in love with airplanes. He studied aeronautical engineering and designed gliders and other aircraft. He earned a pilot's license and then became fascinated with space travel after studying the work of Russian rocket pioneer Konstantin Tsiolkovsky. Korolev became a very talented and hardworking rocket designer.

The Soviet military became interested in Korolev's experiments with liquid-fueled rockets. He worked for the government, designing rockets that could carry weapons or people into space.

In 1938, Korolev was falsely accused by the Soviet Union of sabotaging the government's rocket program. This was part of the Soviet Union's "Great Terror." Millions of people suspected of being enemies of the government were killed or imprisoned. Korolev was tortured and exiled to faraway Siberia.

When World War II ended in 1945, the Soviet Union realized it needed rocket designers to help it understand seized German V-2s. Korolev was released and ordered to work with captured German rocket engineers as well as Soviet scientists.

In the coming years, Korolev became a colonel in the Red Army, and the head rocket and spacecraft engineer of the Soviet Union. His identity was kept top secret. To the outside world, he was known only as the "Chief Designer." He was responsible for many long-range Soviet missiles, satellites, and manned spacecraft. It was only after Korolev's death in 1966 that his true identity was revealed as the most important Soviet rocket designer of the Space Race.

CHAPTER 8
THE COLD WAR

THE DEMOCRATIC UNITED STATES AND THE COMMUNIST SOVIET Union had very different kinds of governments. They distrusted each other. They competed in many ways, especially with their militaries. Without actually going to war against each other, they spent vast amounts of money to develop new and powerful weapons. This "Cold War" saw competition in unexpected places, including space.

Out of the ashes of World War II, the United States and the Soviet Union emerged as the world's two superpowers. During the war, they seemed to be equals. But in 1945, America used nuclear bombs against Japan. These frightening weapons tipped the balance of power. After the war, Soviet leader Joseph Stalin was determined to get nuclear bombs for his own country, and find ways to fire them quickly across the oceans. The Soviets detonated their first nuclear bomb in 1949. People in the United States were shocked. Next would come a race in missile technology between the two countries, and a rush into space to show the world once and for all which country was the most powerful.

CHAPTER 9
THE ICBM

IN THE OPENING DAYS OF THE COLD WAR, BOTH THE UNITED STATES and the Soviet Union had nuclear bombs. They were the most fearsome, destructive weapons ever invented. The next step was to find a way to drop the bombs on the enemy in the quickest, most devastating way possible.

Building on the success of the German V-2, each country worked hard to improve its missile technology. They strived to deliver nuclear warheads anywhere in the world, and to strike so quickly there would be no time to defend or retaliate.

The American and Soviet militaries realized that learning to travel in space would help them reach their goals. What they raced to build were powerful new missiles called ICBMs.

ICBM stands for "intercontinental ballistic missile." "Intercontinental" means it can travel into space and then strike a faraway continent. For example, an ICBM launched from Asia could strike North America. "Ballistic" means that once the warhead is released, it falls back to Earth using gravity, like a ball tossed to the ground from a tall building. Modern ICBMs have a minimum range of about 3,400 miles (5,472 km).

The world's first ICBM came from the Soviet Union. It was the R-7 Semyorka, which was designed by the Soviet's chief rocket scientist Sergei Korolev. First successfully launched in 1957, it could deliver a single nuclear bomb up to 5,500 miles (8,851 km) away. At 112 feet (34 m) tall, it used liquid-fuel engines, including four boosters strapped around a larger, central rocket. The R-7's basic design is still used today.

ICBM research started later in the United States. The American military believed it could handle any threat with its fleet of long-range bomber aircraft. Making new missiles wasn't a top priority. That changed in the early 1950s when the Soviet Union exploded its first atomic bombs. The Americans raced to catch up.

The first American ICBM was the Atlas missile. The first successful flight was in 1958. The Atlas was 85 feet (26 m) tall. Like the Soviet R-7, its engine was powered by liquid fuel. It could strike a target up to 9,000 miles (14,484 km) away with its single nuclear warhead.

Research and testing of military missiles later helped human space exploration. Powerful ICBMs were sometimes used in manned spaceflight missions. Instead of carrying bombs, they were altered to carry capsules with astronauts or cosmonauts riding inside.

Soviet cosmonaut Yuri Gagarin, the first human to travel into space and orbit the Earth, was carried aloft by an R-7-style rocket. And astronaut Alan Shepard, the first American in space, rode a modified military Redstone missile that boosted his Mercury spacecraft into the history books.

CHAPTER 10
SPUTNIK

MANY HISTORY BOOKS MARK OCTOBER 4, 1957, AS THE BEGINNING OF the Space Race. On that date in the Soviet Union, a mighty R-7 rocket, designed by Sergei Korolev, rode a fireball into the night sky. When it reached the edges of space, instead of dropping a bomb, it released a beach-ball-sized metal sphere with four long antennae.

The mysterious object was called Sputnik 1. It was the first satellite made by humans to orbit the Earth. Sputnik 1 was an artificial moon. Its name translated to "fellow traveler."

The Soviet Union kept Sputnik 1's launch a secret. When the Soviet government revealed its presence, people were shocked, especially in the United States. The small satellite weighed 184 pounds (83 kg) and measured about 23 inches (58 cm) in diameter. It traveled around the Earth every 98 minutes, broadcasting a simple beeping radio signal as it sped along its elliptical orbit.

The Soviets had beaten the Americans into space and into Earth orbit. But how could such a small, beeping object cause such fear?

Two years before Sputnik was launched, in 1955, President Dwight Eisenhower announced that the United States would take part in a scientific event called the International Geophysical Year.

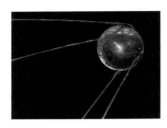

The Soviet Union launched Sputnik 1 on October 4, 1957. The small, unmanned satellite transmitted a radio signal for 22 days.

It was to be an 18-month project from 1957 to 1958. Scientists from more than 60 countries would exchange ideas and research. President Eisenhower said the US would contribute by launching the world's first Earth-orbiting satellite. It would be used for peaceful, scientific research. It would also show the world the superiority of American technology.

German missile designer Wernher von Braun, who now worked for the American government, was happy with the news. He and his team had been working on a powerful new rocket called Redstone. It could easily boost a satellite into Earth orbit.

Unfortunately for Wernher von Braun, his Redstone rocket was rejected. Instead, the US Navy's Vanguard rocket was chosen to hoist the first American satellite into orbit.

Meanwhile, in the Soviet Union, rocket designer Sergei Korolev argued that his country should also launch a satellite, and do it before the United States. Soviet leader Nikita Khrushchev agreed that such a project would prove that the Soviet Union, not America, was superior.

By 1957, Vanguard was far behind schedule. Wernher von Braun pleaded with the government to launch his Redstone rocket with a satellite payload, but his proposal was rejected. While the Americans delayed, the Soviets were ready to shock the world.

On October 4, 1957, the Soviet Union launched Sputnik 1 into orbit. It was stunning news around the world. This was a time when people in the United States and many other countries were suspicious of the Soviet Union. Until this time, most people were sure the United States was the most advanced country on Earth. But Sputnik 1 gave astonishing proof that the Soviets were just as technologically advanced, maybe even more so. Any ham radio operator could hear Sputnik 1's *"beep... beep... beep..."* when it sailed overhead. People could also simply look up with binoculars or a telescope and see the shiny silver ball as it moved across the night sky.

Some Americans looked up at Sputnik 1 in wonder. Astronauts Alan Shepard and Deke Slayton, as well as spacecraft designer Harrison Storms, were inspired to pursue careers in space exploration.

On November 3, 1957, the Soviets amazed the world again with the successful launch of Sputnik 2. This time, the satellite carried several scientific instruments, as well as a dog named Laika. The Soviets proved that a living creature could survive being launched into space (although Laika died a few hours later).

Many Americans were fearful. Now that the Soviets had put the first satellites into orbit, what would they do next? Could they use satellites to spy on the United States? Could they even drop nuclear bombs down on unsuspecting American cities? The Space Race had suddenly become very real and very serious.

CHAPTER 11
AMERICA'S TURN

THE UNITED STATES GOVERNMENT WAS CAUGHT OFF GUARD BY THE Soviet Union's "October Surprise." Sputnik 1 and Sputnik 2 were stunning scientific achievements. The satellites were also frightening reminders of how quickly the Soviet Union had become a real superpower capable of attacking the United States. The American public demanded to know how the United States had fallen so far behind its Cold War rival in science and technology. How long would it be before the Soviets could launch a surprise nuclear attack on the United States? Could America ever catch up in the Space Race?

President Eisenhower ordered the Navy to launch a satellite on its Vanguard rocket as soon as possible. He wanted to calm fearful Americans and reassure them that the United States continued to have the best technology. The launch would even be shown live on television.

On December 6, 1957, the Vanguard rocket lifted off from its launchpad at Florida's Cape Canaveral. Unfortunately, the launch did not go as planned. The 75-foot (23-m) tall, 3-stage rocket rose a few inches and then hovered in the air for a moment. It finally sank back to Earth and exploded in an enormous fireball. The satellite was ejected from the top of the rocket and landed in some nearby bushes. Though damaged, it began forlornly transmitting its radio signals.

The Vanguard rocket failure was a terrible embarrassment to the United States. The country's space program seemed to be a mess compared to the Soviet Union. People were losing confidence in the government. After Vanguard's launchpad explosion, newspaper headlines across the country screamed "Flopnik!" and "Kaputnik!" At last, the government realized that Wernher von Braun's Redstone rocket was America's best chance to catch up to the Soviets. Von Braun and his team of scientists were ordered to prepare for launch.

The Redstone was a 69-foot (21-m) -tall, single-stage rocket. Designed by the military, its primary job was to carry nuclear weapons. On January 31, 1958, a modified Redstone perched on a launch pad at Florida's Cape Canaveral. This version was called Juno 1. Instead of carrying a nuclear bomb, it held a satellite called Explorer 1.

When the countdown clock reached zero, the Juno 1 rocket lifted off flawlessly. Once it reached space, Explorer 1 was successfully released. America had finally put an artificial satellite into orbit around Earth. Explorer 1 contained several scientific instruments. Some searched for cosmic radiation. The Explorer program eventually discovered the Van Allen Belts, which are large zones of radioactive particles that circle the Earth.

The Soviet Sputnik crisis resulted in many changes in the United States. New satellites were launched, and math and science were given more importance in schools. The US government also put more effort into space exploration. On October 1, 1958, the National Aeronautics and Space Administration (NASA) was created. It took over for the old National Advisory Committee for Aeronautics (NACA). NASA would be responsible for all civilian space programs. The country's space exploration efforts would be more unified and streamlined. With any luck, the United States would keep up with, and maybe even outshine, its Cold War rival the Soviet Union.

CHAPTER 12
HIGH-FLYING SPIES

LAUNCHING NUCLEAR MISSILES OR SCIENTIFIC SATELLITES WERE NOT the only reasons to explore space. The United States military had another very important goal: to spy on the Soviet Union and other countries from high above.

Spy satellites, also called reconnaissance satellites, are used by the military to observe an enemy's bases, cities, and armed forces. This can be extremely useful when planning for war. It also helps the government decide how much money to spend on military equipment in order to respond to an enemy threat.

In the late 1950s, the Air Force's U-2 spy plane was used to take pictures of the Soviet Union's military forces. It flew at an altitude of 70,000 feet (21,336 m), which was too high to be shot down. But by 1960, the Soviets invented new missiles that could reach the high-flying U-2.

On May 1, 1960, a U-2 piloted by Captain Francis Gary Powers was shot down over the Soviet Union. Powers worked for the US Central Intelligence Agency (CIA). His capture by the Soviets created an international crisis.

Powers was eventually set free. But even before the crisis began, the United States knew it needed a better way to keep track of the Soviet military. With the Space Race already begun, the military found what it was looking for: spy satellites.

Shortly after the Soviet Union launched Sputnik 1 in 1958, US President Dwight Eisenhower signed an order that created a top-secret program. It would be run by the CIA and the Air Force. Its mission was to launch satellites that could take photographs of Soviet military bases and other targets. The photographs would then be retrieved after landing back on Earth in a heat-shielded capsule. The spy satellites were named Corona (code-named Discoverer).

A United States Air Force U-2 spy plane.

Most Corona satellite cameras used black-and-white film. Each satellite could carry thousands of feet of film. On early missions, the cameras could see objects on the ground about 40 feet (12 m) across or bigger. As technology improved, the cameras detected objects as small as three feet (.9 m) in diameter.

The first successful Corona satellite was launched in August 1960. For the next 12 years, over 100 Corona missions were flown. Combined, they took more than 800,000 photographs of the Soviet Union, China, and other hostile countries. The first photograph from space of Soviet territory revealed an air base in Siberia. That same mission revealed more territory in the Soviet Union than all the U-2 spy planes combined.

When a Corona mission was complete, the nose cone of the satellite was ejected and a return capsule fell to Earth. A shield protected the film from the intense heat of reentry through the atmosphere. A radio signal told operators its location. As the capsule neared the surface, a parachute was released, slowing its descent. A special recovery aircraft swooped in and snatched it out of midair.

The Corona program was very effective. It helped the United

States discover a great deal about the Soviet military. In the late 1950s, Americans feared there was a "missile gap" between the two counties. The Soviets were believed to have a far greater number of missiles than the United States. The Corona spy satellites proved the opposite was true: the United States had more missiles. This knowledge helped ease the fear of a surprise Soviet missile attack.

PROJECT MERCURY

CHAPTER 13
PROJECT MERCURY

ON OCTOBER 4, 1957, THE SOVIET UNION LAUNCHED SPUTNIK 1, THE first artificial satellite to orbit the Earth. Americans were shocked. Future US president Lyndon B. Johnson said, "Now, somehow, in some new way, the sky seemed almost alien. I also remember the profound shock… it might be possible for another nation to achieve technological superiority over this great country of ours."

Three months after Sputnik, the United States responded with a satellite of its own: Explorer 1. The space race had begun.

The National Aeronautics and Space Administration (NASA) began work on October 1, 1958. Its first big job was Project Mercury. There were three primary goals: put a manned spacecraft in orbit; make sure astronauts could live in space; get the astronauts safely back home.

NASA had thousands of scientists and technicians working on rockets and other hardware. Now it needed to find astronauts.

A Mercury-Redstone rocket launches Alan Shepard in his *Freedom 7* capsule into space on May 5, 1961.

CHAPTER 14
THE MERCURY 7

PROJECT MERCURY'S PRIMARY MISSION WAS TO PUT THE FIRST Americans in space. In January 1959, NASA began looking for pilots with "the right stuff," as author Tom Wolfe later wrote. The space agency decided that the first group of astronauts should be test pilots. That meant they needed considerable experience with the most advanced aircraft ever built. They needed to be smart and to stay calm during emergencies. They also had to work well as a team, and think quickly on their own. There were physical requirements, too. Each astronaut had to stand less than 5 feet, 11 inches tall (1.8 m), and weigh under 180 pounds (82 kg).

NASA received more than 500 applications for the job. Those accepted for initial testing went through a grueling series of physical and mental evaluations.

At the end of this process, just seven astronauts were chosen. They were announced to much public fanfare as the "Mercury 7." They included Alan Shepard, Gus Grissom, Gordon Cooper, Wally Schirra (Shuh-RAH), Deke Slayton, John Glenn, and Scott Carpenter.

CHAPTER 15
THE MERCURY SPACECRAFT

THE MERCURY SPACECRAFT, OR CAPSULE, WAS BUILT TO CARRY JUST one astronaut. Inside the tiny compartment, he would be strapped into his seat the entire flight. The spacecraft contained dozens of electronic switches and mechanical levers needed to control its flight path. There was no computer on board. Landings and other maneuvers were calculated by computers on Earth and then sent by radio.

The Mercury capsule had to protect the astronaut from the harsh vacuum of space. That meant there needed to be enough air, heat, food, and water for the duration of the flight. If the compartment developed a leak, the occupant inside would quickly suffocate and die.

NASA mechanical engineer Max Faget designed the Mercury spacecraft. The cone-shaped capsule measured about seven feet (2.1 m) long and six feet (1.8 m) in diameter. Affixed to the top was a rocket-propelled launch escape tower. It was built to carry the capsule to safety in case of an explosion or other catastrophe.

The bottom of the capsule was blunt. It contained a heat shield to keep the astronaut safe during reentry. Before landing, the spacecraft fell through the Earth's atmosphere at over 17,500 miles per hour (28,164 kph). Friction generated by flying through air at that speed caused the heat shield temperature to rise to 3,000 degrees Fahrenheit (1,649°C). Without a way to deflect the heat, an astronaut inside would fry to a crisp. If all went well, parachutes would deploy and the capsule would land safely in the ocean, where it would swiftly be picked up by waiting recovery crews.

John Glenn's Friendship 7 Mercury spacecraft.

CHAPTER 16
ANIMALS IN SPACE

IN ORDER TO MAKE THE MERCURY SPACECRAFT SAFE FOR ASTRONAUTS to fly, NASA tested the rockets and electronic systems many times. These test flights were conducted without people aboard. Sometimes, the test worked flawlessly. Other times, the rockets exploded, or systems failed. On one test flight, the emergency launch escape tower flew off into the sky, leaving the capsule sitting atop its lifeless rocket. Then, comically, the capsule's parachute popped out and fell to the ground.

Whether a test flight failed or succeeded, the engineers and designers learned something new about the Mercury spacecraft so it could be improved. But to make sure the system was safe for humans, animals were launched inside Mercury capsules before the astronauts.

Some doctors questioned whether humans could withstand long periods of weightlessness, not to mention the tremendous strain of lifting off and landing. There were also concerns about radiation exposure. To test these matters without endangering human astronauts, both the Soviet Union and the United States had previously sent animals into space or high altitudes. The most common creatures tested were mice, dogs, monkeys, and chimpanzees. The Soviets preferred dogs, while the Americans tested several monkeys and chimps.

Aboard the Soviet Union's Sputnik 2 satellite was a dog named Laika. She was a stray picked up from the streets of Moscow. On November 3, 1957, she became the first dog in space and the first living creature to orbit the Earth. Sadly, after several orbits, Laika died of overheating.

Before the first manned Mercury mission, scientists wanted a test flight with an animal aboard. The astronauts were unhappy about the delay, but NASA decided it was a necessary precaution. On January 31, 1961, Ham became the first chimpanzee in space. There were some technical failures, but Ham survived. During his 16-minute flight, he experienced almost 7 minutes of weightlessness. After a safe landing, a physical exam showed no major problems from his flight. The delay, however, gave the Soviet Union a chance to beat the Americans into space.

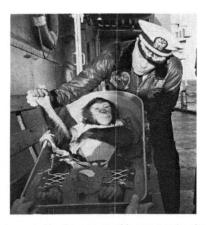

Ham is greeted by the recovery ship commander after his flight on a Mercury-Redstone rocket in 1961.

CHAPTER 17
YURI GAGARIN

ASTRONAUT ALAN SHEPARD WAS PREPARED TO BE THE FIRST HUMAN launched into space. But after the Mercury spacecraft's technical problems with the chimp Ham aboard, NASA insisted on one last unmanned test flight for safety. Shepard fumed. He was convinced he could handle any problems that might arise. Plus, the delay might give the Soviets a chance to launch a cosmonaut and beat the Americans. Unfortunately, Shepard was proven right.

On the morning of April 12, 1961, 27-year-old cosmonaut Yuri Gagarin stood next to an R-7 rocket at the Baikonur Cosmodrome in remote Kazakhstan, Soviet Union. Gagarin had trained as a pilot and cosmonaut all his adult life for this moment.

Gagarin rode the thundering R-7 toward the heavens. "Poyekhali!" ("Let's go!") he cried in excitement. Inside his Vostok 1 spacecraft, named *Swallow*, he could feel jolts and bumps and hear loud bangs as the rocket fell away, its fuel spent. Gagarin was now streaking through space at 17,500 miles per hour (28,164 kph), faster than any human had ever traveled. He soared high above the Earth, maxing out at 203 miles (327 km) in altitude. Gagarin had done it! He had become the first person in space.

After one complete orbit, Vostok 1 began its descent. Gagarin was shielded from the heat of reentry through Earth's thick atmosphere. Before hitting the ground, he was ejected from the spacecraft and parachuted safely down, startling two peasants working in a farm field.

Yuri Gagarin.

As Gagarin gathered his parachute, one woman asked him, "Have you come from space?"

Gagarin replied, grinning, "Yes! I certainly have!"

After his historic flight, Yuri Gagarin received the title "Hero of the Soviet Union," the nation's highest honor.

CHAPTER 18
FREEDOM 7

WHEN ASTRONAUT ALAN SHEPARD HEARD THE NEWS THAT YURI Gagarin had become the first man in space, he was disappointed and angry, along with most Americans. The country's newly elected president, John F. Kennedy, even considered canceling the Mercury program. What was the point of spending so much money and endangering lives if the Soviet Union had already won the race to space? But Kennedy soon changed his mind, insisting that NASA continue its work. "Space," he said, "is our great new frontier." He was determined to catch up to the Soviets and surpass them, knowing the huge political reward in demonstrating the superiority of America's space technology. Just three weeks after Gagarin's flight, NASA was ready to fulfill the president's challenge.

In the early morning darkness of May 5, 1961, Alan Shepard, wearing his silvery spacesuit, walked toward the Redstone rocket with the Mercury capsule mounted on top, six stories above him. He leaned back and craned his helmeted head upward, taking one last look before entering the elevator that would whisk him to his spacecraft, which he had named *Freedom 7* (the number "7" was used to honor the teamwork of the original seven Mercury astronauts).

Alan Shepard.

After waving to his launch team, the elevator whisked Shepard to the top of the rocket, where he was strapped into his custom-fitted seat inside the Mercury spacecraft. The hatch was sealed, and then he waited. The tiny compartment left little wiggle room. Shepard noticed a sign taped to the instrument panel. It read, "No handball playing in here." Shepard looked through the spacecraft's window and saw fellow astronaut John Glenn grinning at him. Shepard gave Glenn a thumbs-up. The ground crew was soon evacuated, and the world watched as the countdown began.

Then the clock stopped. A problem had developed with the spacecraft's hardware. The issue was eventually fixed, and the countdown clock restarted. Then it stopped again. For several hours, technicians worked to fix problems as they cropped up. Finally, Shepard had enough. He radioed, "Why don't you just fix your little problem and *light this candle?*"

BATHROOM BREAK

Shepard's flight was only supposed to last 15 minutes. But because of long delays, he was forced to sit on the launchpad for hours. Nature inevitably took its course. He radioed fellow astronaut Gordon "Gordo" Cooper at Mission Control.

"Man, I gotta pee."

"You what?"

"You heard me. I've got to pee. I've been in here forever!"

After much discussion with NASA engineers, Mission Control gave Shepard permission to relieve himself.

"Do it in the suit," Cooper radioed.

The ground crew heard a long "Ahhhhh" from Shepard on the radio. There was fear that the extra moisture might cause trouble with the spacecraft's electronics, but the urine was absorbed by Shepard's long cotton underwear, and then evaporated in the capsule's 100 percent oxygen atmosphere.

Finally, at 9:34 a.m., the Redstone rocket thundered off the launchpad. Strong vibrations rattled the spacecraft, and a loud roar filled the air. Shepard was squeezed into his seat as G-forces pressed against his body. The rocket performed perfectly. "All systems are go," Shepard radioed. The Redstone engine shut down, and the spacecraft separated from the rocket.

Less than five minutes into the flight, *Freedom 7* reached a height of 116.5 miles (188 km) above the ground. Shepard had become the first American to fly in space.

As the *Freedom 7* spacecraft floated high above Earth, Shepard could feel the weightlessness of space. He only had a few minutes to enjoy it. He took over manual control of the spacecraft so he could test how well it turned and rolled. For the first time, a human being was actually *flying* a spacecraft, which was more than Yuri Gagarin could boast. (The Soviet capsule had been automatically controlled.)

Soon, *Freedom 7* turned. Retrorockets fired and Shepard began his plunge back to Earth. His suborbital spaceflight lasted 15 minutes, 22 seconds before he splashed down in the Atlantic Ocean. He was quickly plucked from the water and returned home a national hero.

CHAPTER 19
KENNEDY'S CHALLENGE

ALAN SHEPARD RECEIVED A HERO'S WELCOME AFTER RETURNING FROM his historic mission. Most Americans now supported NASA's manned spaceflight program. President John F. Kennedy knew that space exploration, and especially beating the Soviets, would help unify the American people. Winning the Space Race would show the world that America, not the Soviet Union, had the best technology and brainpower.

President Kennedy got advice from Vice President Lyndon B. Johnson, who was very active in the government's space program. Kennedy also consulted with scientists, politicians, and military leaders. On May 25, 1961, he gave a speech to Congress to unveil his vision of America's role in space exploration.

"I believe this nation," Kennedy said, "should commit itself to achieving the goal, before the decade is out, of landing a man on the Moon and returning him safely to Earth. No single space project in this period will be more impressive to mankind, or more important for the long-range exploration of space, and none will be so difficult or expensive to accomplish."

Kennedy's address was met with enthusiasm by most people. On September 12, 1962, he gave another speech, this time at Rice Stadium in Houston, Texas. He explained America's goal of reaching the Moon: "We set sail on this new sea because there is new knowledge to be gained, and new rights to be won, and they must be won and used for the progress of all people... We choose to go to the Moon! We choose to go to the Moon in this decade and do the other things, not because they are easy, but because they are hard; because that goal will serve to organize and measure the best of our energies and skills, because that challenge is one that we are willing to accept, one we are unwilling to postpone, and one we intend to win... ."

CHAPTER 20
LIBERTY BELL 7

By late July 1961, nearly two months had passed since President John F. Kennedy's "landing a man on the Moon" speech to Congress. It was almost three months after Alan Shepard's historic flight aboard *Freedom 7*. The public eagerly awaited the next American achievement in space.

On July 21, 1961, astronaut Virgil "Gus" Grissom felt the Redstone rocket ignite under his *Liberty Bell 7* spacecraft. The Air Force test pilot pressed back in his seat as the acceleration (G-forces) made him feel several times heavier than his normal body weight. Vibrations inside the capsule grew more severe as the spacecraft rocketed upward. Eventually, the violence of the launch subsided. Grissom could feel the Redstone run out of fuel. Explosive charges separated the spent rocket from the Mercury spacecraft.

Through *Liberty Bell 7's* new, larger window, Grissom watched as the color of the Earth's horizon changed from dark blue to black. He felt the eerie sense of weightlessness come over him. About three minutes after launch, Gus Grissom became the second American to fly in space.

After Alan Shepard's *Freedom 7* flight, several design changes were made to Grissom's *Liberty Bell 7* spacecraft. The two small portholes were replaced with a large trapezoid-shaped window that made it easier to see the exterior of the spacecraft and witness the world as it turned below. There was also a hastily designed urine collector to avoid the embarrassment Alan Shepard suffered during his mission. The biggest change was to the capsule's hatch. Instead of a hand-operated mechanism, explosive bolts were added so the astronaut could escape quickly in an emergency.

Gus Grissom is helped into his *Liberty Bell 7* spacecraft by fellow astronaut John Glenn.

Grissom enjoyed the feeling of weightlessness in the middle of his short flight. He was also fascinated by the views of Earth through the spacecraft's window. He said, "I could make out brilliant gradations of color, the blue of the water, the white of the beaches, and the brown of the land."

Grissom forced himself to return to the business of flying his spacecraft and monitoring its electronic systems. The flight of *Liberty Bell 7* was meant to be a repeat of Alan Shepard's mission. It would be suborbital, lasting about 15 minutes from launch to splashdown. The spacecraft would make a high arc in the sky, entering the weightlessness of space for a few minutes before falling back to Earth.

At last, Grissom felt the spacecraft's retrorockets fire, which allowed *Liberty Bell 7* to begin its descent. Everything went as planned. When he splashed down in the Atlantic Ocean—about 300 miles (483 km) from the launchpad—Grissom had been aloft for exactly 15 minutes and 37 seconds.

As recovery helicopters hovered nearby, Grissom heard a loud thud—the explosive hatch had blown open. Water began pouring into the capsule. The astronaut nearly drowned, but he narrowly escaped. After long minutes treading water, he was hoisted to safety by a rescue helicopter. However, the *Liberty Bell 7* spacecraft sank to the bottom of the Atlantic, 15,000 feet (4,572 m) beneath the waves.

The reason the hatch blew remains a mystery. The best explanation to date is that an electrical arc caused by a cutting tool surged through the cabin and caused the explosive bolts to detonate. (The co-pilot of the helicopter leaned out and snipped *Liberty Bell 7*'s long antenna, making the capsule safer to latch onto.) Whatever the explanation, NASA cleared Grissom of any wrongdoing. The incident reminded the astronauts and the public of just how dangerous space travel could be, even after returning to Earth.

CHAPTER 21
FRIENDSHIP 7

By mid-1961, two American astronauts had flown into space. Both Alan Shepard and Gus Grissom had taken suborbital "hops" of about 15 minutes each. But America still seemed to be losing the Space Race. After all, on the Soviet Union's first attempt, cosmonaut Yuri Gagarin had not only traveled beyond the atmosphere, but had orbited the Earth as well.

NASA's Redstone rocket simply wasn't powerful enough to lift the heavy Mercury capsule into orbit. The space agency decided to switch rockets. It modified an Air Force missile called Atlas. Unfortunately, several Atlas test flights exploded. The next Mercury mission would be filled with danger. NASA had the perfect astronaut in mind for the job: John Glenn.

Glenn was a US Marine Corps combat pilot and war hero. As a test pilot, he broke many aviation speed and distance records. He was fearless, cool under pressure, and one of the best pilots in the country. If anybody had "the right stuff," it was John Glenn. But before Glenn's rocket was ready for liftoff, the Soviet Union had another surprise in store for the Americans.

On August 6, 1961, 25-year-old cosmonaut Gherman Titov (the youngest person ever to fly in space) blasted off in his Vostok 2 spacecraft. The flight was a success, even though Titov suffered terribly from space sickness. He circled the Earth nearly 18 times during a mission that lasted a full day. The Soviet achievement made NASA even more determined to put an astronaut in orbit around the Earth.

On February 20, 1962, John Glenn sat inside his *Friendship 7* spacecraft. The capsule was mounted atop a gleaming-silver Atlas rocket at Florida's Cape Canaveral. The mission had been delayed for several days because of bad weather and mechanical problems, but on this morning, all systems were go.

As the clock wound down, fellow astronaut Scott Carpenter called out on the radio, "Godspeed, John Glenn."

The countdown continued. "Three... two... one... zero! Roger, the clock is operating, we're underway!" Flames poured from the Atlas's engines. The spacecraft slowly rose, and then accelerated. The sound of thunder crackled through the air. Teeth-rattling vibrations shook the rocket. Metal groaned and shrieked. "It's a little bumpy along here," radioed Glenn.

Friendship 7 lifts off.

In a few minutes, the ride settled down. After the Atlas booster fell away, the Mercury spacecraft was over 100 miles (161 km) high and traveling 17,300 miles per hour (27,842 kph). Free of Earth's gravity now, Glenn radioed back, "Zero-G and I feel fine. Capsule is turning around. Oh, that view is tremendous!" John Glenn was in orbit around Earth. America was finally catching up in the Space Race.

As the world turned under *Friendship 7*, John Glenn described what he was seeing to the millions of people glued to their radios and televisions. From high above, he saw snow-covered mountains and the deep hues of the oceans. He saw the tops of thunderclouds flashing. Three times, the spacecraft traveled from day into night. Once, while entering sunrise, he witnessed thousands of tiny lights floating around the capsule, like a swarm of fireflies. (They were later discovered to be ice crystals that had been knocked loose from the capsule's exterior surface and were now drifting free and glinting in the sunlight.)

After the first orbit around Earth, one of the thrusters that controlled *Friendship 7* became stuck. Glenn was forced to fly manually, but this was no obstacle for the well-trained pilot.

A warning light appeared on Glenn's control panel. Apparently, the capsule's heat shield had come loose. Without the shield, the astronaut would be incinerated when *Friendship 7* reentered the atmosphere. At first, NASA kept the problem a secret so Glenn could continue his tasks without worry, but they eventually told him the alarming truth. His flight was cut short as plans were made to help him survive.

John Glenn during his historic flight.

During reentry, Glenn was ordered to keep the spacecraft's retrorockets strapped to the bottom of the heat shield, instead of jettisoning them as planned. With any luck, the straps would keep the heat shield from jarring completely free.

As he hurtled through the atmosphere at supersonic speed, Glenn saw the spacecraft become enveloped in a fireball. Bits of burning metal flew past the window. Was it his heat shield burning up?

There were tense moments at Mission Control as *Friendship 7* passed through the blackout zone. This was the part of reentry when radio waves couldn't reach the spacecraft because of hot gasses surrounding the capsule. Finally, after long minutes of worry, they could hear Glenn's voice crackle on the radio. He was alive! (Later, an investigation determined that the heat shield warning light had been a simple malfunction.)

After four hours, 55 minutes, and 23 seconds of flight, Glenn splashed down safely in the Atlantic Ocean. When a doctor asked him if he had noticed any unusual activity during his historic mission, the astronaut responded, "No, just a normal day in space."

CHAPTER 22
MERCURY SPACESUITS

ALL THE MERCURY ASTRONAUTS WORE SPACESUITS THAT WERE A modified version of the US Navy Mark IV suit. The Navy Mark IV was made for pilots who flew jets at very high altitudes.

The silver-colored Mercury spacesuits fit an astronaut's entire body. They were custom-fitted for each astronaut, and could be pressurized in an emergency if the spacecraft ever had a leak and lost air pressure. Air mixed with oxygen could be pumped inside the sealed suit to create pressure, which would allow the astronaut to breathe. The Mercury suits had a breathing system that let in oxygen through a tube connected near the astronaut's waist. Air circulated through the suit and then exited through another tube in the astronaut's helmet. The system was also designed to keep the astronauts cool. None of the Mercury flights ever lost pressure inside the capsule, so the astronauts' pressure suits were never inflated.

The outer shell was nylon that was coated with silvery aluminum. This helped control the astronauts' temperature. Safety boots were also coated. Gloves had curved fingers to help grip spaceflight controls, but the middle finger was straightened and stiffened. This helped the astronauts press switches on the instrument panels. Otherwise, they had to grasp and push the switches with a small stick, which was more awkward.

Mercury astronaut Gordon Cooper in his custom-fitted pressure suit.

CHAPTER 23
AURORA 7

JOHN GLENN'S *FRIENDSHIP 7* FLIGHT PROVED THAT THE MERCURY spacecraft could keep an astronaut alive, even when orbiting the Earth. The basic questions had been settled. Long exposure to weightlessness was not immediately dangerous, and reentry into Earth's atmosphere could be safely accomplished. It was time to learn more about space.

The Mercury-Atlas 7 mission was originally assigned to Deke Slayton. However, doctors detected an irregular heartbeat during a physical and grounded him. Scott Carpenter was ordered to take his place. Slayton became responsible for astronaut training and crew assignments.

Carpenter launched in *Aurora 7* on May 24, 1962. Like John Glenn, he orbited the Earth three times. Besides flying his *Aurora 7* spacecraft, he was given several science experiments to perform. He observed how liquids behaved in weightlessness, and photographed sunsets and cloud formations on Earth. He also tried eating solid food, but it crumbled and turned into a hazard to the spacecraft's delicate electronics.

After three orbits, it was time to go home. Because of equipment failure, Carpenter had trouble aligning the spacecraft properly for reentry. In the confusion, he accidentally activated the retrorockets three seconds too late. That tiny error resulted in *Aurora 7* splashing down in the Atlantic Ocean almost 300 miles (483 km) from its target. This caused a scare, but he was found in less than 40 minutes and then safely rescued by the US Navy.

CHAPTER 24
HUMAN COMPUTERS

MATH AND SPACE GO HAND IN HAND. WITHOUT MATH, THERE WOULD be no spacecraft or rockets. To create these machines, space scientists and aeronautical engineers today use electronic computers to perform millions of calculations without error.

In the early days of space exploration, between the 1940s and early 1960s, there were no advanced computers. Engineers still had to prove their theories, but there was so much math to perform that nobody could accomplish it on their own. Instead, these complex mathematical calculations were done by hand, by people called human computers.

Human computers were men and women who solved math problems with their brains, sometimes with the help of complex types of mechanical adding machines. Complicated formulas were broken down into parts and figured out separately. Working together, large groups of human computers could calculate the position of the moon and planets, or the direction a rocket might take if it were pointed a certain way and burned a certain amount of fuel.

In its early days, NASA employed hundreds of human computers to solve the complex engineering problems of sending

HUMAN COMPUTERS

spacecraft into orbit. Most of these people were women, including a large number of African Americans. These positions were often the only way for women with talent and education in mathematics to find work at that time in history. Many were responsible for the math needed to achieve the success of Project Mercury.

Katherine Johnson was a NASA mathematician and physicist. Her life and work were seen in the 2016 film *Hidden Figures*.

CHAPTER 25
SIGMA 7

ASTRONAUT WALLY SCHIRRA BLASTED OFF IN HIS *SIGMA 7* MERCURY spacecraft on October 3, 1962. Pressure was on NASA to accomplish a longer flight than either *Friendship 7* or *Aurora 7*'s three orbits. Schirra was scheduled to complete a much longer mission of six orbits.

Part of the reason the space agency wanted a long-duration flight was that the Soviet Union in mid-August completed two nearly simultaneous missions, Vostok 3 and Vostok 4, each lasting several days. The US, it seemed, was always trying to catch up to the Soviets.

Schirra was a highly skilled pilot and astronaut. During his nine-hour, six-orbit flight, he performed many science experiments and tested new equipment. He pushed *Sigma 7*'s navigation controls to their limits, yet conserved fuel with a precision that surprised controllers back on Earth.

Schirra guided *Sigma 7* through reentry nine hours and 13 minutes after liftoff. The spacecraft splashed down in the Pacific Ocean near Hawaii. Amazingly, it landed just one-half mile (.8 km) from the Navy aircraft carrier USS *Kearsarge*.

It had been a textbook orbital operation, with no major problems. Schirra had flown the longest of any American astronaut so far. He called *Sigma 7* his "sweet little bird." Many in NASA dubbed the mission the "perfect flight."

CHAPTER 26
FAITH 7

Gordon Cooper was called a "hotshot" by some at NASA. He could be brash, and his Oklahoma twang irritated some. But he was a brilliant Air Force pilot, and as it turned out, just the right astronaut for the job of flying the Mercury spacecraft he named *Faith 7*.

Cooper lifted off from Florida's Cape Canaveral on May 15, 1963. During his 34-hour, 22-orbit mission, he flew "higher, farther, and longer" than any Mercury astronaut before him.

Cooper conducted several science experiments during his flight and photographed the distant Earth. He became the first American to sleep in space during the long voyage. He was also the last American to go into space alone.

As the flight came to an end, the overworked spacecraft began to malfunction. *Faith 7* lost much of its electrical power, and the automatic control system died. Cooper reentered Earth's atmosphere by firing the retrorockets manually. He used his wristwatch to time the rockets and drew diagrams on the window to make sure the spacecraft was properly lined up. Cooper was so skilled as a pilot that despite these problems, which might have killed another astronaut, *Faith 7* landed safely just four miles (6 km) from the recovery target in the Pacific Ocean.

FAITH 7

Faith 7 was the very last Mercury mission. NASA had learned much from Project Mercury. It put astronauts in orbit around Earth and discovered how people could work in space. Much of this knowledge would be used in later spaceflights, especially the next step in the Space Race: Project Gemini.

Faith 7 lifts off with Gordon Cooper aboard, the last American astronaut to go into space alone.

PROJECT GEMINI

CHAPTER 27
PROJECT GEMINI

On May 25, 1961, United States President John F. Kennedy unveiled his vision of America's role in space exploration. He called for the National Aeronautics and Space Administration (NASA) to land a man on the Moon "before the decade is out."

It was a bold challenge. The Mercury spaceflights ended in the spring of 1963. NASA learned how to put astronauts into orbit, and how to survive and function in space. But there was still much work to be done before anyone dared travel to the Moon.

NASA created Project Gemini to follow Project Mercury. The space agency needed to find out if astronauts could survive a long lunar voyage. They would also have to dock spacecraft together and work in the harsh vacuum of space if they were to fulfill President Kennedy's dream. Project Gemini was a way to bridge the gap between the successes of Project Mercury and the eventual triumph of the Apollo Moon landings.

Gemini 7 orbits the Earth with astronauts Frank Borman and Jim Lovell aboard. Gemini 7 rendezvoused with Gemini 6A on December 15, 1965. Gemini 6A's crew included Wally Schirra and Tom Stafford.

CHAPTER 28
THE SPACE RACE HEATS UP

BY 1963, THE SPACE RACE WAS IN FULL SWING. WITH PROJECT Mercury, the United States had almost caught up to the Soviet Union. Project Gemini, if all went according to plan, would be the most ambitious undertaking in space exploration in history. But the Soviets refused to sit still. Their secretive program had some surprises in store for the Americans.

On June 14, 1963, the Soviet spacecraft Vostok 5 was sent into orbit. Vostok 6 blasted off two days later. The twin spacecraft flew within three miles (5 km) of each other to test how difficult it might be to rendezvous. However, the biggest surprise was the cosmonaut aboard Vostok 6—Valentina Tereshkova, the first woman in space. The Communist Soviet Union wanted to show that its system treated men and women equally (even though Tereshkova faced a barrage of sexism from the Soviet space program). The United States wouldn't send a female astronaut to space for two decades until Sally Ride's historic mission in 1983.

The Soviets kept up the pressure to outmatch Project Gemini. Spacecraft engineer Sergei Korolev redesigned the interior of the old Vostok capsule to create a roomier version called Voskhod 1. On October 12, 1964, it lifted off with three cosmonauts aboard, the most occupants of any spacecraft so far. And on March 18, 1965, cosmonaut Alexey Leonov became the first person to spacewalk when he floated free outside his Voskhod 2 capsule.

The Americans had a lot of catching up to do with Project Gemini if they wanted to win the Space Race.

Cosmonaut Alexey Leonov exited his Voskhod 2 capsule through a fabric airlock to walk in space on March 18, 1965. After about eight minutes of tethered floating, Leonov realized that his spacesuit was ballooning out. He was now too big to fit in the airlock. Luckily, he was able to slowly vent air from his suit and forcefully pull himself back in.

CHAPTER 29
THE GEMINI SPACECRAFT

The Gemini spacecraft got its name from the constellation Gemini in the night sky. (In the Latin language, the word means "twins.") NASA chose the name because it carried two astronauts. It resembled the Mercury capsule that came before it, but it was bigger. A pair of astronauts fit inside, even though it was a tight squeeze. Two were required to test long-duration flights, and to practice docking with other spacecraft. Both skills would be needed to fly to the Moon.

Gemini was roughly 18 feet (5.5-m) long, and had two main parts. The front cabin where the astronauts sat was called the reentry module. It was the only part designed to return safely to Earth. It was built with a heat shield on the bottom that protected the astronauts from the tremendous heat generated by traveling through the atmosphere at high speed during reentry. The detachable rear of the spacecraft was called the adapter section. It carried oxygen, water, fuel, electrical power, and other essentials needed for the mission.

Unlike earlier Mercury spacecraft, Gemini had an onboard computer to help the astronauts maneuver through space. It also had radar and an artificial horizon instrument so they could fly in full manual control if necessary.

Several of the original Mercury 7 were picked to fly in the Gemini spacecraft. Joining them was batch of new crewmates. Some of these men would go down in history as the greatest astronauts who ever lived, including John Young, Ed White, and Neil Armstrong.

Gemini was sent into orbit atop a Titan II GLV rocket. It was a modified version of a nuclear missile used by the US Air Force.

CHAPTER 30
GEMINI 3

Gemini 3 was the first mission to carry astronauts. Gemini 1 and 2 were unmanned flights to make sure all systems were as safe as possible. NASA scientists tested the capsules' electronics, flight stability, and heat shields on reentry. After two successful launches, the spacecraft design was approved for live astronauts to begin flying.

On March 23, 1965, at Florida's Cape Canaveral, astronauts Virgil "Gus" Grissom and John Young were strapped into their tight-fitting seats inside their Gemini spacecraft. Underneath the capsule was a towering Titan II rocket, ready for liftoff. This was Grissom's second spaceflight, after his Mercury mission in 1961. Rookie John Young had never been to space, but he was a highly skilled US Navy test pilot who held several speed and altitude records.

Gemini 3 was a "shakedown" mission that tested the spacecraft's systems and flight controls. Grissom and Young's job was to find out if anything needed fixing or adjusting before future flights began. Unlike the Mercury capsule, Gemini was maneuverable in space. It could change the direction of its orbit and its altitude above Earth.

Gus Grissom named the capsule *Molly Brown*, after a survivor of the *Titanic* cruise ship disaster in 1912. Her nickname was "unsinkable." The name playfully referred to Grissom's Mercury *Liberty Bell 7* capsule, which accidentally filled with seawater and sank in the Atlantic Ocean after splashdown.

Gemini 3 lifts off.

The Gemini 3 countdown reached zero at 9:24 a.m. Fire belched from the Titan II rocket like flames shooting from a dragon's mouth. It rose in the air, slowly at first, until it cleared the launchpad, then steadily gained speed. The astronauts were pressed back in their seats as the acceleration (G-forces) made them feel several times heavier than their actual body weight. When the second stage of the rocket ran out of fuel, the Gemini capsule separated and the astronauts felt the weightlessness of space travel. At the highest part of its orbit, the spacecraft was 140 miles (225 km) above Earth, traveling at about 17,500 miles per hour (28,164 kph).

Gemini 3 completed three orbits in a flight lasting 4 hours, 52 minutes. Grissom and Young checked all spacecraft systems, took photos of the Earth, and performed a series of science experiments, one of which investigated the effects of zero gravity on how cells divide.

During their third orbit, Grissom and Young tested the spacecraft's new propulsion system. They fired thrusters that slowly changed the capsule's course. For the first time in history, a spacecraft changed its altitude and direction of travel. These were critical maneuvers that needed to be mastered before astronauts could venture to the moon.

The Gemini 3 flight was mostly uneventful. Grissom and Young said the spacecraft handled "like a pilot's delight." After safely splashing down in the Atlantic Ocean, they were picked up by recovery crews from the US Navy aircraft carrier USS *Intrepid*.

Gemini 3 Pilot John Young (left) and Commander Gus Grissom inside the *Molly Brown* capsule.

CHAPTER 31
GEMINI 4

GEMINI 4 WAS FLOWN BY TWO ROOKIE ASTRONAUTS, JAMES "JIM" McDivitt and Edward "Ed" White. The four-day mission was to prove that humans could live and work in zero gravity for long periods of time. It would be the first time American astronauts stayed in orbit for several days.

NASA had always planned to have an astronaut walk in space, but it was supposed to happen much later in the Gemini program. However, after the Soviet Union's Alexey Leonov floated outside his spacecraft in the world's first spacewalk three months earlier, NASA changed its schedule. America couldn't be seen as falling far behind the Soviets. The space agency told McDivitt and White to begin training for a spacewalk. The two astronauts worked well together and quickly learned the procedures for an extravehicular activity (EVA). White was chosen for the dangerous task of venturing outside the capsule.

McDivitt and White blasted off from Cape Canaveral on June 3, 1965, just 10 weeks after the previous Gemini 3 mission. Gemini 4's main purpose was to test the performance of the spacecraft during its long, four-day flight. It would be the first to be guided by the new Mission Control Center in Houston, Texas (located at today's Johnson Space Center).

After liftoff, the smooth ride up was interrupted only by the explosive separation of stage one and stage two of the Titan II rocket. When stage two shut down and the capsule separated, the astronauts entered weightlessness at an orbit of 180 miles (290 km) at its high point above Earth.

Soon after the second-stage booster separated, McDivitt steered the spacecraft so that it was facing backward. They searched for the spent booster and spotted it trailing a few hundred feet away. One of the astronauts' first jobs was to practice a rendezvous with another object in space. It was a task that needed to be perfected for Moon missions.

McDivitt aimed the capsule at the booster and thrust toward it. Strangely, the spent rocket seemed to move downward and farther away. McDivitt tried again, with the same result. In order to save fuel, Ground Control ordered him to give up chasing the booster.

What the astronauts and Ground Control didn't understand at the time was something called "orbital mechanics." It is a way objects behave in orbit. By firing the thrusters, McDivitt caused his spacecraft to increase speed, which raised the height of its orbit. This made it slow down compared to the booster. That explained why the booster seemed to travel faster and farther away, no matter how many times McDivitt used the thrusters.

With the orbital rendezvous abandoned, McDivitt and White prepared for the most dangerous part of their mission—space-walking.

Three orbits into Gemini 4's flight, the crew started depressurizing the inside of the spacecraft. Gemini didn't have a clumsy fabric airlock like Soviet capsules. Instead, both American astronauts sealed their spacesuits. When given the go-ahead by Mission Control, Ed White opened the hatch above him, exposing both men to the vacuum of space.

White's spacesuit insulation shielded him from extreme temperatures. Anything facing the Sun reached 250 degrees Fahrenheit (121°C). When White drifted into the spacecraft's shadow, temperatures plunged to -150 degrees Fahrenheit (-101°C). His helmet's visor was gold-plated to protect his eyes from glare.

White checked his equipment. He had a 25-foot (8-m) tether that gave him a steady flow of oxygen. It was also designed to prevent him from drifting away from the ship.

White used a handheld "zip gun" to push himself away from the capsule. It held pressurized oxygen. Brief spurts helped him move in space, just like a miniature rocket.

The feeling of floating freely in space delighted White. He marveled at the views of Earth. He stood on Gemini 4's titanium hull and grinned, then pushed off again and floated around the spacecraft. "This is the greatest experience," he said to McDivitt. "It's just tremendous."

Finally, Ground Control ordered White to return to the capsule. The astronaut wanted more time for spacewalking, but Ground Control was firm. "The flight director said get back in," McDivitt told White.

White said it was the saddest moment of his life.

After struggling to squeeze back into his seat and shut the stubborn hatch, America's first spacewalk came to an end. White's total time outside the capsule was about 20 minutes.

The rest of the mission went smoothly. On June 7, 1965, Gemini 4 splashed down safely in the Atlantic Ocean. Ed White and James McDivitt were quickly picked up by the US Navy aircraft carrier USS *Wasp*. The astronauts' four-day, 66-orbit flight broke a record for the longest American spaceflight to date.

Ed White, America's first spacewalker, during his extravehicular activity (EVA) of the Gemini 4 mission. "It's just tremendous," White said of spacewalking.

CHAPTER 32
GEMINI 5

The crew of Gemini 5 included Project Mercury veteran Gordon "Gordo" Cooper and Navy test pilot Charles "Pete" Conrad, who was new to the astronaut corps. Cooper would become the first person ever to fly an Earth orbital mission twice.

Gemini 5's goal was to assess rendezvous and navigation systems on the spacecraft. It would also try to stay in orbit for eight days, doubling Gemini 4's endurance record.

Gemini 5 lifted off from Florida's Cape Canaveral on August 21, 1965. It was a smooth ride to space, except for the rough jolts when the Titan II's two stages ran out of fuel and separated. When Gemini 5 was clear of stage two, the astronauts experienced weightlessness. They went into orbit at a maximum height of 207 miles (333 km) above the Earth.

Gemini 5 used new fuel cells instead of short-lived batteries to generate electricity. Batteries could only last a few days at most. Fuel cells made electricity for as long as fuel and oxygen were available. They would be necessary for long trips to the Moon. Although Gemini 5's fuel cells malfunctioned mid-flight, they generated enough electricity to continue the full mission.

Cooper and Conrad performed many science experiments inside their cramped spacecraft. Probes monitored their body functions, including blood pressure and eyesight, to check for the effects of weightlessness. The astronauts tested Gemini 5's navigation system. They also photographed stars and Earth landmarks as they passed over.

The astronauts battled boredom over the long mission. The cabin was so confined that Conrad joked it was like spending "eight days in a garbage can." He wished he'd brought a book along to read. One day, the monotony was broken at mealtime when the astronauts had an accident with freeze-dried shrimp, resulting in tiny weightless crustaceans filling the cabin.

After 7 days, 22 hours, and 55 minutes in orbit, Cooper and Conrad splashed down safely in the Atlantic Ocean. They had broken the Soviet endurance record in space, and proved that humans could survive in good health on a long trip to the Moon and back.

SPACE FOOD

On long missions, the Gemini astronauts were given packets of dehydrated food. The water was removed beforehand to save space and weight. Some dishes included beef and gravy, or fruit such as peaches. The crew prepared the food by injecting water into the plastic packets. They then squished the packets with their fingers until it was mixed together. Gemini missions also included some ready-to-eat foods wrapped in foil or plastic, such as chicken sandwiches or cubes of cereal and cinnamon toast.

CHAPTER 33
RENDEZVOUS: GEMINI 6A AND 7

The first three crewed missions of Project Gemini demonstrated that the spacecraft and the astronauts could function during long flights. Now it was time to tackle another goal: learning how to dock two spacecraft together while in orbit, a critical skill for later Moon missions. During a trip to the Moon, the main command module, the capsule in which the astronauts would live during the journey, needed to be docked to a lunar lander. Once orbit was established around the Moon, the lander would undock from the command module, descend to the surface, and then return, attaching itself to the command module once more. But before any of that could happen, astronauts had to learn how to fly two spacecraft near each other without colliding. Lacking a safe rendezvous, there could be no successful Moon landing.

Gemini 6 was meant to intercept an unmanned spacecraft already in orbit and practice docking with it. The two astronauts in the Gemini capsule were Wally Schirra and Tom Stafford. The other spacecraft was called an Agena Target Docking Vehicle. Gemini 6 and the Agena were scheduled to launch on the same day, October 25, 1965. The Agena went first. Unfortunately, it exploded a few minutes after launch, and the Gemini 6 mission was scrubbed.

Next in line was Gemini 7. It lifted off on December 4, 1965. Its crew included astronauts Frank Borman and Jim Lovell. Their mission was to spend nearly two full weeks in space, testing the long-term effects of weightlessness on the human body. The astronauts also performed several science experiments.

The mission became tedious for the crew, despite the books they had brought with them. The capsule was cramped and overheated, even when they took off their spacesuits to sleep.

December 15 was Borman and Lovell's 11th day in orbit. A pair of visitors finally broke their boredom. Astronauts Wally Schirra and Tom Stafford arrived in their renamed Gemini 6A spacecraft. Instead of launching another unmanned Agena vehicle, NASA had decided to have the two Gemini capsules rendezvous. They were not equipped to dock with each other, but could practice close maneuvering.

Schirra and Stafford, aboard Gemini 6A, tracked Gemini 7 on a newly installed radar unit. The two spacecraft used their maneuvering thrusters to move next to each other. For over four hours, they flew around one another and side by side, sometimes as close as one foot (.3 m) apart.

After the successful rendezvous mission, Schirra and Stafford splashed down in the Atlantic Ocean on December 16, 1965. Borman and Lovell followed in Gemini 7 two days later. They had been in space for 13 days and 18 hours, a new endurance record.

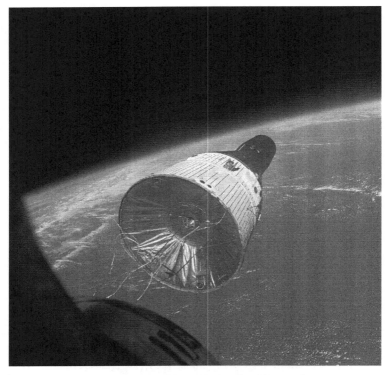

This historic photo was taken from Gemini 6A when Gemini 7 was about 37 feet (11 m) away.

CHAPTER 34
GEMINI 8

THE GEMINI 6A AND 7 FLIGHTS PROVED TWO SPACECRAFT COULD rendezvous and fly side by side. However, one very important part of spaceflight had yet to be achieved: docking.

On March 16, 1966, NASA launched another unmanned Agena. Gemini 8's task was to rendezvous and dock with it, a repeat of the original Gemini 6 mission, but hopefully this time without the drama of a spacecraft blowing up.

The Gemini 8 crew included Neil Armstrong and David "Dave" Scott. (Armstrong would later become the first person to walk on the Moon, in 1969.) Both astronauts were eager to travel into space, having trained for years for the job. They lifted off atop their Titan II rocket one hour and 41 minutes after the Agena launch, unaware of the near tragedy awaiting them.

Shortly after liftoff, Armstrong and Scott spied the Agena. It took Gemini 8 just five hours to catch up. The astronauts flew around the 26-foot (7.9-m) long spacecraft, inspecting it for any launch damage. Everything seemed fine.

Armstrong positioned Gemini 8 so that its nose aligned with the docking collar on one end of the Agena. He waited for the message from Ground Control to proceed. "Okay, Gemini 8," Houston radioed up to them. "You're looking good… go ahead and dock."

Armstrong nudged the capsule forward. The astronauts felt a slight bump, and then heard electric motors whirring and clicking as the two spacecraft latched onto each other. Armstrong radioed the news to Houston. "Flight, we are docked. It's really a smoothie."

Gemini 8 had successfully caught up to another orbiting vessel and docked. It was the first time in history that two spacecraft had linked together in orbit around Earth. The milestone proved that future Moon landing missions were possible.

Shortly after the triumph of docking, however, serious trouble arose. While temporarily out of radio contact with Houston, Gemini 8 began rotating rapidly. Armstrong and Scott struggled to control their spacecraft. They suspected something was wrong with the Agena, so they flew manually and undocked. That just made the tumbling worse.

When they regained contact with Ground Control, Scott relayed news of the emergency. "We have serious problems here," he said. "We're tumbling end over end. We're disengaged from the Agena."

Surprised controllers in Houston asked what kind of problem they were having. Armstrong chimed in, "We're rolling and we can't turn anything off." What they didn't know was that there was an electrical problem in one of Gemini 8's maneuvering thrusters. A short circuit caused it to fire continuously, creating an accelerating rate of spin.

Gemini 8's smooth mission had turned into a nightmare. Armstrong, a former Naval aviator and test pilot, used all his skills to counter the roll. The spacecraft had seemingly gone berserk. At one point, they were rotating more than one revolution per second. The astronauts' vision blurred, and they almost fainted from the strain. The spacecraft was in danger of breaking apart.

In a last-ditch effort, Armstrong disengaged the entire maneuvering thruster system. He switched to the re-entry thrusters on the nose of the spacecraft and fought to regain control. Finally, after nearly 30 minutes of terror, Armstrong stopped the spin. He had used an alarming 75 percent of their re-entry propellant.

Following safety protocols, Houston ordered the astronauts to abort the mission and return to Earth. After completing a sixth orbit, they splashed down safely in the Pacific Ocean. Their cool thinking under pressure saved their lives. The Gemini 8 mission was a success, but it reminded everyone of just how risky space travel could be.

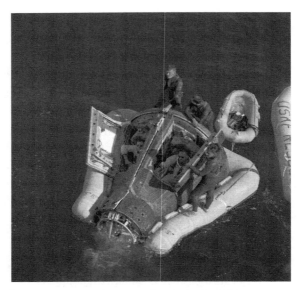

During a terrifying ride on a malfunctioning Gemini 8, astronauts Neil Armstrong and David Scott used all their piloting skills to save the mission. They safely splashed down in the Pacific Ocean on March 17, 1966.

CHAPTER 35
GEMINI 9A

TRAGEDY STRUCK THE GEMINI 9 MISSION IN ITS EARLY DAYS. THE original crew included Elliot See and Charles Bassett. On February 28, 1966, they were flying together in a T-38 Talon. Normally based in Houston, Texas, the astronauts were traveling to St. Louis, Missouri, for simulator training at McDonnell Aircraft, one of the companies that made the Gemini spacecraft.

Astronaut See was piloting the two-seater jet. Weather was snowy and foggy that dreary morning in St. Louis. As they descended from the low clouds, See realized he had overshot the airport runway. He pulled up and veered right, striking the roof of a nearby building. Both astronauts died instantly in the fiery crash, and 17 people on the ground were injured.

Soon after the accident, backup crew members Tom Stafford and Gene Cernan were given command of the mission (Stafford had already flown aboard Gemini 6A in December 1965). The spacecraft was renamed Gemini 9A. The astronauts' primary goal was to dock with an unmanned Agena spacecraft, which was to be sent into orbit just before Gemini 9A. Minutes after launch, however, the Agena guidance system failed because of a short circuit. The malfunction caused one of the two Atlas booster engines to pitch downward. The doomed spacecraft crashed into the Atlantic Ocean 90 miles (145 km) from Florida's Cape Canaveral.

A replacement for the Agena was hastily assembled. Slightly smaller and less technologically advanced than its predecessor, it was called the Augmented Target Docking Adapter (ATDA). It was launched on June 1, 1966. Two days later, Stafford and Cernan lifted off from Cape Canaveral, boosted by their Titan II rocket, which sent them into orbit 170 miles (274 km) above the Earth.

Three orbits after liftoff, Cernan and Stafford rendezvoused with the ATDA. There was a surprise waiting for them when they closed to within a few miles of the other spacecraft.

"That's a weird-looking machine," Stafford radioed to Mission Control. A protective cover on the front of the ATDA was designed to split into two parts and fall away from the spacecraft after it achieved orbit. However, incorrectly installed straps kept the cover stuck to the ATDA's base. "It looks like an angry alligator," said Stafford.

The malfunctioning cover blocked the Gemini spacecraft from docking. Ground Control and the astronauts briefly considered trying to knock the shroud off manually, either with a spacewalk or by nudging it with the Gemini capsule, but that idea was deemed too dangerous for the crew.

Even though NASA called off the docking procedure, the astronauts gained experience by repeatedly moving away from the ATDA and then maneuvering close to it again. They simulated what it would be like for a lunar landing vehicle to rendezvous with a command module.

Besides flight practice, Gene Cernan also ventured outside the capsule for a two-hour spacewalk. The dazzling views of Earth amazed him, but his assigned tasks soon made him grow fatigued. He had trouble maneuvering in his stiff spacesuit, and he sweated so much that his visor fogged over. He finally retreated to the safety of the spacecraft, totally exhausted. Working in space was apparently more difficult than it first appeared to be.

Gemini 9A returned to Earth on June 6, 1966, after completing 47 orbits. The astronauts splashed down in the Atlantic Ocean, less than one mile (1.6 km) from the US Navy aircraft carrier USS *Wasp*.

CHAPTER 36
GEMINI 10

GEMINI 10 WAS LAUNCHED INTO SPACE ON JULY 18, 1966. ITS THREE-day mission was filled with science experiments, spacewalks, and a double docking test. It was the most complex flight yet. All the lessons learned were necessary stepping stones for later trips to the Moon.

Astronauts John Young and Michael Collins had a busy schedule. Their first task was to dock with an Agena unmanned spacecraft. After docking, they used the Agena's own engine to alter their orbit. They climbed to an altitude of 474 miles (763 km) above Earth. It was the highest any astronauts had ever flown.

Gemini 10 remained docked with the Agena for 39 hours. After lowering their altitude, they detached from the unmanned spacecraft. Their next task was to perform another rendezvous with a second Agena, the same one left behind by Gemini 8.

Collins performed two EVAs (extravehicular activities) on the mission. The first time, he simply stood up in the open hatch. He took photographs of stars for about six minutes. Later, Collins floated over to the second Agena spacecraft and retrieved a micrometeorite experiment that was attached to the hull.

Collins had difficulty working in weightlessness. It was hard to move in the stiff spacesuit. He kept sliding off the sides of the

Agena and Gemini spacecraft. There were no handholds to grip. After his last spacewalk, it took Collins eight minutes to close the hatch and seal the cabin.

Gemini 10 splashed down in the Atlantic Ocean after completing 43 orbits. The crew was picked up by the US Navy ship USS *Guadalcanal*.

CHAPTER 37
GEMINI 11

GEMINI 11 WAS A THREE-DAY MISSION TO RENDEZVOUS AND DOCK with an Agena unmanned spacecraft. Spacewalks and science experiments were also scheduled. Astronauts Pete Conrad and Richard "Dick" Gordon lifted off from Cape Canaveral on September 12, 1966.

Conrad and Gordon docked with the Agena just 1 hour and 38 minutes after launch. It was the first time a spacecraft had docked with another on its first orbit. During the three-day mission, the spacecraft would practice docking five times.

Conrad and Gordon used the Agena's engine to boost their spacecraft into a higher orbit. They broke Gemini 10's altitude record by climbing to 850 miles (1,368 km) above the Earth, higher than any manned spacecraft had ever flown. It was about four times higher than today's International Space Station (ISS).

Gordon performed two EVAs (extravehicular activities), the first of which was troublesome. While floating outside to perform work on the capsule's exterior, he quickly grew tired working in weightlessness. His helmet frosted over, and he almost couldn't see to return to Gemini 11. The spacewalk was cut short because of the danger. The second EVA was easier. Gordon simply stood up in the open hatch and photographed the Earth and stars for about two hours.

Gemini 11 separated from the Agena spacecraft after a total docking time of two days, 30 minutes. After 44 orbits, Conrad and Gordon splashed down in the Atlantic Ocean, just two miles (3 km) from the planned landing zone.

Although Gemini 11 was a success, NASA was worried that it hadn't yet solved the troubles of spacewalking. It was a problem that needed to be worked out if astronauts were ever to make it safely to the Moon.

CHAPTER 38
GEMINI 12

GEMINI 12 WAS THE TENTH AND FINAL MANNED FLIGHT OF PROJECT Gemini. It launched on November 11, 1966, carrying astronauts Jim Lovell and Edwin "Buzz" Aldrin. On their third orbit, they successfully intercepted and docked with an unmanned Agena spacecraft. However, their primary goal was to finally prove that humans could work outside the capsule without becoming overheated or exhausted.

Gemini astronauts often trained in a large KC-135 airplane nicknamed the "vomit comet." By flying up and down in a wide arc, it created weightless conditions during dives for about 30 seconds at a time, which crews could use to simulate spacewalking.

Besides the KC-135, NASA arranged underwater training for the Gemini 12 crew. A mock-up capsule was submerged in a large swimming pool. Buzz Aldrin used counterweights on his suit to achieve "neutral buoyancy," which simulated weightlessness. This lasted longer and was more helpful than the vomit comet.

From lessons learned during his work in the pool, Aldrin ordered footholds and handrails that he installed on the outer surface of the Gemini 12 capsule and Agena during his first stand-up spacewalk. He devised wrist tethers that prevented tools from floating away, and foot restraints resembling wooden shoes that could be bolted to certain places on the hull. He also invented portable handholds that could be attached to either spacecraft. These would help keep his body steady in zero gravity. Tools were kept in special protective pockets in his spacesuit.

Aldrin spacewalked for a total of five hours, 38 minutes. With regular intervals of rest, he made it seem easy compared to previous missions. He scooted along the capsule with hardly any effort. His breathing and heartbeat remained normal. His helmet did not frost over from frozen sweat and breath. He proved astronauts could work outside their spacecraft for long periods of time.

After four days and 59 orbits around the Earth, Gemini 12 safely splashed down in the Atlantic Ocean. Lovell and Aldrin were picked up by recovery crews from the US Navy aircraft carrier USS *Wasp*.

Project Gemini catapulted the American space program far ahead of the Soviet Union. But the Space Race continued. Project Apollo was already underway. The next step was the biggest prize of all: the Moon.

During his first spacewalk on November 12, 1966, Buzz Aldrin set his camera on the edge of the open hatch and took what he called "the first space selfie," with Earth in the background.

PROJECT APOLLO

CHAPTER 39
THE FIRST FOOTSTEPS ON THE MOON

On July 20, 1969, American astronauts Neil Armstrong and Buzz Aldrin became the first humans to land on the Moon. It was the climax of the Space Race, a fierce competition between the United States and the Soviet Union (much of which is today's Russia).

Project Apollo built on the successes of the Mercury and Gemini programs. Apollo spanned more than a decade and was overseen by three presidents. The cost to the nation was more than $25 billion. Tragically, three astronauts lost their lives in a launchpad fire in 1967.

Despite all the hardships, landing astronauts on the Moon gave America tremendous prestige in the eyes of the world. Project Apollo advanced science and gave us new technology. It also fulfilled a dream as old as humanity: to send people to the Moon and bring them safely back to Earth.

A close-up view of astronaut Buzz Aldrin's bootprint in the lunar soil, taken during the Apollo 11 crew's landing and exploration of the Moon in 1969.

CHAPTER 40
MOON PROBES

APOLLO 11 LANDED ON THE MOON IN 1969, BUT THE NATIONAL Aeronautics and Space Administration (NASA) tried for many years beforehand to learn as much as possible about our closest celestial neighbor. Even by the late 1950s, scientists knew surprisingly little, only that there was no air to breathe, and no water to drink. Most of the lunar surface was a mystery. There were no detailed maps, and the far side of the Moon (the side that always faces away from Earth) had yet to be seen by any satellite.

Along with NASA, the Soviet Union's space program was also hard at work trying to find out about the Moon. The Soviets and Americans were locked in the Space Race. The country with the most data would have an enormous advantage when it came time to land a manned spacecraft on the lunar surface.

Between 1958 and 1969, the two countries sent dozens of probes and landers. Most crashed or missed completely. An early success was the Soviet Union's Luna 2. On September 13, 1959, the probe intentionally impacted on the surface, becoming the first human-made object to reach the Moon.

The Soviets bragged that, once again, they possessed the superior space program. By this time, the closest NASA had come was a flyby of the Pioneer 4 space probe, which had approached within 37,282 miles (60,000 km). Just a few weeks after Luna 2, the Soviet Union's Luna 3 took the first pictures of the far side of the Moon. On February 3, 1966, Luna 9 became the first probe to achieve a soft landing and send back images, proving that a lander would not sink into the dusty lunar soil.

Despite the early Soviet successes, the United States persevered. In 1964 and 1965, the Ranger 7, 8, and 9 probes took detailed photos of the Moon before crashing into the surface. Images were radioed back to Earth before they crashed. Maps made from the photos helped pick the sites for the later manned Apollo missions.

On June 2, 1966, NASA's Surveyor 1 made a soft landing on the Moon. It was the first of several American Surveyor landers. They took pictures and gathered information about the lunar surface, and even took soil samples.

CHAPTER 41
MONSTER ROCKETS

THE SATURN V ("SATURN FIVE") ROCKETS USED FOR THE APOLLO missions to the Moon were the biggest, most powerful ever made. Sometimes nicknamed "monster rockets," they were designed by chief rocket engineer Wernher von Braun. He was a German-born scientist who worked for the United States after World War II. Von Braun and his team took six years to develop the complicated Saturn V.

Rocket engineer Wernher von Braun next to a set of Saturn V engines.

The three-stage Saturn V towered 363 feet (111 m) high, nearly 60 feet (18 m) taller than the Statue of Liberty on its pedestal. It weighed 6.2 million pounds (2.8 million kg) fully fueled. The first stage produced 7.6 million pounds (3.4 million kg) of thrust during a two-minute burn, enough to launch the weight of 10 school busses into orbit. Its five massive engines together gulped up to 20 tons (18 metric tons) of liquid fuel per second. The Saturn V had more than enough power to send three astronauts and their heavy spacecraft to the Moon.

While the Americans worked on the Saturn V, the Soviet Union was busy building a monster rocket of its own. It was called the N-1. Like the Saturn V, it had three stages. The brainchild of the Soviet's chief rocket designer, Sergei Korolev, the N-1 was slightly shorter than the Saturn V, but its cluster of engines could produce more thrust. Unfortunately for the Soviets, each of the four unmanned N-1 launch attempts failed when the rockets either burst into flames or exploded. The N-1 failures delayed the Soviet Moon program for several years.

CHAPTER 42
THE APOLLO SPACECRAFT

AMERICAN ASTRONAUTS TRAVELED TO THE MOON IN A SPACECRAFT comprising three main parts, or modules. The crew spent most of their time in the command module. This conically shaped capsule was significantly larger than the earlier Mercury or Gemini spacecraft. Three astronauts had room enough to move around and stretch when their seats were folded up. It was about as spacious as the interior of a large car.

The command module was covered with a heat shield, thickest at the bottom, that protected the crew during the fiery reentry through Earth's atmosphere. To cushion the impact of landing, three large parachutes opened at the top just before splashdown in the ocean.

Attached to the rear of the command module was the cylinder-shaped service module. It held fuel for the voyage, fuel cells that made electricity, plus many scientific instruments. In back was the spacecraft's main rocket engine. The service module was separated from the command module shortly before reentry.

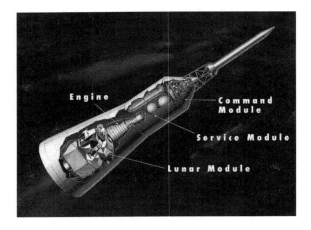

The part of the spacecraft that landed on the Moon was called the lunar module. It had four legs that extended outward, with large pads on the ends to keep it from sinking into the lunar dust. The lunar module had two parts. When the Moon exploration was finished, only the top part returned to dock with the orbiting command module.

The lunar module was small inside, with room for two astronauts. It was their base during surface explorations, with enough oxygen and other supplies for about a three-day mission.

CHAPTER 43
A TRIP TO THE MOON

When planning how to send astronauts to the Moon, NASA chose a "lunar orbit rendezvous" type of flight. Instead of sending a gigantic rocket to land on the Moon and then return in one piece, the Apollo spacecraft was modular. Each part had a different job. Only the small lunar module landed on the surface. That meant not as much fuel needed to be carried all the way from Earth. With a modular system, however, docking and undocking could be hazardous. But NASA decided it was worth the risk in order to avoid designing and building a larger rocket than necessary.

MISSION CONTROL

Although most of the manned Apollo flights lifted off from the Kennedy Space Center on Merritt Island in Florida, once launched, they were overseen by Mission Control in Houston, Texas. Housed in Building 30 of today's Johnson Space Center, it was the workplace for dozens of flight controllers, computer technicians, and scientists during the Apollo missions. Apollo spacecraft were constantly tracked and monitored, and when trouble arose, it was up to Mission Control to help find solutions.

CHAPTER 44
APOLLO 1 TRAGEDY

February 21, 1967, was supposed to be the date of the first Apollo mission. Tragically, Apollo 1 ended before it even got off the ground. During a preflight test on January 27, a spark ignited the pure-oxygen atmosphere of the command module. A flash fire raged inside the enclosed capsule, and astronauts Virgil "Gus" Grissom, Edward "Ed" White, and Roger Chaffee were killed within seconds.

Gus Grissom had flown on two previous missions, one Mercury and one Gemini. In 1961, in his Mercury Liberty Bell 7 spacecraft, he became the second American astronaut to travel to space. Ed White, like Grissom, was a veteran of the Gemini program. He was the first American spacewalker, an achievement he earned during the Gemini 4 mission in 1965. Roger Chaffee was a decorated US Navy pilot. Apollo 1 would have been his first trip to space.

After the Apollo 1 launchpad fire, manned flights were suspended for almost two years. At a cost of millions of dollars and three precious lives, the tragedy resulted in a major redesign of the command module, with better safety and testing procedures.

APOLLO 1 TRAGEDY

The crew of Apollo 1, from left to right: Virgil "Gus" Grissom, Edward "Ed" White, and Roger Chaffee.

CHAPTER 45
SOYEZ 1

As NASA mourned the loss of three astronauts in the Apollo 1 fire, the Soviet Union found itself with a disaster of its own. By 1967, the Soviets had developed a new generation of spacecraft called Soyuz. It could change the direction of its orbit and dock with other spacecraft, like NASA's Gemini. However, Soyuz was also designed to go all the way to the Moon.

Unmanned Soyuz test launches had uncovered many problems. The system wasn't fully ready. But when the Apollo 1 tragedy struck, Soviet leader Leonid Brezhnev saw a chance for his space program to shine.

The Soviets planned to launch a Soyuz spacecraft into orbit with a single cosmonaut aboard. A day later, three more cosmonauts would lift off in a second Soyuz. After a rendezvous and docking in space, two of the cosmonauts would switch spacecraft. Brezhnev was sure the complicated and dangerous mission would show the world the superiority of the Communist government. Engineers warned their leaders that Soyuz wasn't ready, but their concerns were ignored.

The cosmonaut chosen to fly Soyuz 1 was Vladimir Komarov. He lifted off from the Baikonur Cosmodrome space center in Kazakhstan on April 23, 1967. Komarov's problems began soon after launch. One of Soyuz 1's solar panels did not unfold, and the spacecraft's flight system was unstable.

The next day, thunderstorms prevented Soyuz 2 from lifting off. There would be no rendezvous. Meanwhile, high above Earth, Komarov was having more trouble with Soyuz 1. Finally, the mission was aborted, and he was ordered to begin reentry after a little more than a day in orbit.

As Komarov plummeted through the atmosphere, he could barely control Soyuz 1. Then, the main parachute failed to open. Horrified onlookers watched as the spacecraft slammed into the ground at nearly 400 miles per hour (644 km/hr) and burst into flames. Komarov died instantly.

Cosmonauts didn't fly in space again until 18 months after the Soyuz 1 tragedy. The Soyuz capsule was redesigned and made safer (although three more cosmonauts perished in the Soyuz 11 accident in 1971). With such a long delay, the Soviet Union fell further behind the Americans in the race to the Moon.

CHAPTER 46
APOLLO 7

On October 11, 1968, Apollo 7 lifted off from Cape Canaveral, Florida, rising into space atop a pillar of orange flame. Astronauts Wally Schirra, Walt Cunningham, and Donn Eisele were flying inside a newly redesigned Apollo command module. Boosting them into orbit was a Saturn 1B rocket, a smaller two-stage version of the Saturn V. The larger rocket wasn't needed because the lunar module was left behind. Apollo 7's mission was to test the command and service modules.

Previous unmanned missions included Apollo 4, 5, and 6. (There was no Apollo 2 or 3.) The test flights were all successes, except for an engine failure on Apollo 6. Hopes were high for the first mission with a crew aboard.

As Apollo 7 rose higher into the sky, Schirra radioed to Mission Control in Houston, Texas, "She's riding like a dream." When they were safely in orbit around Earth, the astronauts tested the command module's flight systems, including rendezvous and docking. They also performed science experiments, and broadcast live television images to Earth.

The crew was delighted with the relative spaciousness of the new capsule. The earlier Mercury and Gemini cabins were very cramped, but inside the Apollo spacecraft, the astronauts could unstrap themselves and float freely. There was even a rest area beneath the seats for privacy.

After a successful mission, Apollo 7 splashed down in the Atlantic Ocean on October 22, 1968. They had flown for almost 11 days in orbit, which would have been enough time to get to the Moon and back.

AHCHOO!

The only real problem on the Apollo 7 mission was a terrible cold contracted by Wally Schirra, which he passed on to the other two astronauts. In the weightlessness of space, mucus painfully fills the nasal passages and does not drain from the nose, like on Earth. The only thing they could do was blow their noses hard, which hurt their eardrums. Aspirin and decongestants helped with the pain, but the astronauts grew irritated with each other, and there was tension with Mission Control. They ignored some orders, including one to keep their helmets on during reentry. The crew wanted the ability to clear their noses during the pressure changes of the descent, but NASA denied the request, not knowing the dangers that might arise. The aggravated astronauts flew reentry without their helmets anyway.

Their insubordination ensured that none of Apollo 7's astronauts would ever again fly in space. The mission was a technical success, but it reminded NASA that special attention should be paid to the human factor, especially the effects of stress and temperament.

CHAPTER 47
APOLLO 8

After the success of Apollo 7, NASA had a bold plan for its second manned Apollo mission. The lunar module was not yet fully prepared, so it was too early to actually land on the Moon. However, the US believed the Soviet Union was preparing to send a crewed spacecraft into lunar orbit. The unmanned Soviet Zond 5 probe had already circled the Moon with two tortoises, flies, and mealworms aboard.

The United States badly wanted the first humans in lunar orbit to be Americans, so NASA moved up its launch schedule. Rather than simply testing equipment in Earth orbit, as planned, Apollo 8 would instead travel all the way to the Moon and back. The mission would assess navigation instruments and procedures, knowledge that would set the stage for later Apollo missions.

Apollo 8's crew included Commander Frank Borman, James Lovell, and William Anders. Borman and Lovell previously flew together on Gemini 7. Lovell had also flown on Gemini 12. Apollo 8 was William Anders's first trip to space.

On December 21, 1968, Apollo 8's enormous Saturn V rocket rumbled to life and lifted off from Kennedy Space Center's Launch Pad 39A in Florida. It was the first manned flight of a Saturn V, and all systems were go. After reaching Earth orbit, the crew performed a perfect 17-second burn of the rocket's third stage. The rocket fell away, sending Apollo 8 on its three-day voyage to the Moon.

On the third day, Apollo 8 slipped around the far side of the Moon. All radio contact with Earth was lost during this time. The crew completed a rocket burn that slowed the spacecraft enough to be captured by the Moon's gravity and place it in orbit. If they had made a mistake, Apollo 8 could have been hurled into space forever. There was a tremendous sigh of relief from Mission Control when radio contact resumed, and the crew reported that all was well.

Because they had traveled from Earth with the spacecraft pointed backward, the crew members only now got their first good close-up view of the Moon. Jim Lovell remarked at how gray and colorless the lunar surface appeared. They were all amazed at the number of craters they saw, some of them quite large.

During 20 hours of orbiting the Moon, the crew took detailed photos of the surface. These images would help pinpoint landing sites for future Apollo missions.

On Christmas Eve, the Apollo 8 crew gave an emotional television address to the people back home. They described the black void of space, and the desolation of the Moon. Then each man read a part of the Bible's Book of Genesis about the creation of the Earth. Frank Borman finished the broadcast with these now-famous words: "And from the crew of Apollo 8, we close with good night, good luck, a Merry Christmas and God bless all of you—all of you on the good Earth."

After a three-day return flight, Apollo 8 splashed down safely in the Pacific Ocean on December 27, 1968. Borman, Lovell, and Anders were welcomed home as heroes.

On Christmas Eve, December 24, 1968, as the Apollo 8 astronauts orbited the Moon, they witnessed a wondrous sight. There was the Earth, rising over the Moon's horizon. Photographed by astronaut Bill Anders, the image has come to be known as "Earthrise." Said Anders, "We came all this way to explore the Moon, and the most important thing is that we discovered the Earth."

CHAPTER 48
APOLLO 9

APOLLO 9 LIFTED OFF ON MARCH 3, 1969, ABOUT TWO MONTHS AFTER Apollo 8's historic flight around the Moon. Astronauts James McDivitt, David Scott, and Russell "Rusty" Schweickart stayed closer to home, limited to orbiting Earth. They tested the lunar module to make sure it was safe for Moon missions. It was the first time the lunar module flew with a crew.

When launched, the lunar module was tucked underneath the command module. After the command module was released in orbit, it turned around and docked with the lunar module, pulling it away from its protective shell. The astronauts named their command module *Gumdrop*. The lunar module was called *Spider* because of its odd shape. During the mission, the astronauts flew *Spider* on its own, and simulated a return from the Moon.

The lunar module *Spider* is tested while Apollo 9 is in Earth orbit.

CHAPTER 49
APOLLO 10

APOLLO 10'S MISSION WAS TO ORBIT THE MOON, JUST LIKE APOLLO 8. However, this time, a lunar lander tagged along. The mission was a dress rehearsal for Apollo 11, which was scheduled to land on the Moon later that summer. Apollo 10 lifted off on May 18, 1969. The crew included Thomas Stafford, Gene Cernan, and John Young. They named their command module *Charlie Brown* and the lunar module *Snoopy*.

After achieving orbit around the Moon, Young stayed behind and flew *Charlie Brown*, while Stafford and Cernan descended in *Snoopy*. They came within nine miles (14 km) of the lunar surface before turning back. It was a bittersweet moment for the astronauts to journey so far without actually touching down, but their tests and measurements would be an immense help for the historic Moon landing to come.

CHAPTER 50
APOLLO 11

IN 1961, PRESIDENT JOHN F. KENNEDY CHALLENGED THE NATION TO put astronauts on the Moon before the end of the decade. "No single space project," he said, "will be more impressive to mankind, or more important for the long-range exploration of space, and none will be so difficult or expensive to accomplish."

From left to right: Armstrong, Collins, Aldrin.

On July 16, 1969, the late president's dream was about to come true. On that day, American astronauts Neil Armstrong, Edwin "Buzz" Aldrin, and Michael Collins began their historic Apollo 11 Moon mission. From Florida's Kennedy Space Center, their Saturn V rocket billowed fire and smoke, launching the crew into Earth orbit. Soon, their command module *Columbia* was docked to the lunar module *Eagle*. All was going according to plan. They were beginning a three-day journey that would take them nearly a quarter million miles (402,336 km) to the Moon and a date with history.

On July 20, Armstrong and Aldrin climbed into the lunar module. Apollo 11 had rendezvoused with the Moon and completed 11 orbits in preparation. Now came the moment of truth. After undocking with the command module, the astronauts descended in the *Eagle* toward a spot on the Moon called the Sea of Tranquility. Millions of people on Earth were glued to their radios and televisions, awaiting word of the momentous events unfolding.

| Apollo 11 lifts off.

As Michael Collins piloted the orbiting *Columbia*, Armstrong and Aldrin rode in the cramped cabin of the lunar module, its four insect-like legs extended and ready to land. The astronauts' eyes darted over the panel of glowing buttons and switches in front of them. Word came from Mission Control: "You are go for powered descent."

When they were exactly 50,174 feet (15,293 m) above the Moon and 192 miles (309 km) from the landing site, the astronauts ignited the engine beneath them. Their speed decreased, and the Moon's gravity began pulling them toward the surface.

Eagle's computer guided them down. Armstrong and Aldrin felt the lunar module shake as control thrusters fired automatically, keeping them on course.

A shrill alarm sounded inside the cabin. *Eagle*'s main computer had become overloaded with information. The astronauts prepared to abort, but after some tense moments, Mission Control decided the computer was still working properly and allowed the mission to continue.

When they were 1,300 feet (396 m) above the surface, Armstrong looked out the window and saw they had overshot the landing site. The ground was strewn with boulders. Armstrong took over manual control of *Eagle*. Using all his skills as an astronaut and pilot, he expertly guided the lander to a safer area. Their fuel level was critically low. They were in real danger of crashing.

Finally, after long moments of silence, Mission Control heard Armstrong on the radio, his voice calm and professional: "Houston, Tranquility Base here. The *Eagle* has landed."

About four hours later, Neil Armstrong swung open *Eagle's* hatch. He saw before him a barren, windless lunar landscape under a black sky. He stepped from the lunar module's cabin onto a ladder, then gingerly climbed down each rung, toward a world no human, or any living thing, had ever visited. A TV camera on the side of the lunar lander broadcast Armstrong as he reached the last step.

More than 500 million people on Earth watched as Armstrong seemed to float down to the disk-shaped foot at the end of the lander's leg. (The Moon has just one-sixth the gravity of Earth.) Then, he pressed his left foot carefully into the lunar soil, leaving behind a perfect bootprint. Armstrong spoke into his spacesuit radio. "That's one small step for a man, one giant leap for mankind."

About 20 minutes later, Buzz Aldrin joined Armstrong on the Moon's surface. Before starting their long list of tasks and experiments, the two astronauts took a moment to view the surrounding scene. "It has a very stark beauty all its own," Armstrong said of the crater-pocked landscape. A fine gray powder—Moon dust—covered almost everything.

Buzz Aldrin felt awed by the Moon's gray and tan colors, and the sharp shadows cast by the Sun. "Beautiful, beautiful!" he exclaimed. "Magnificent desolation."

After spending 21 hours on the surface, Armstrong and Aldrin reunited with Michael Collins in *Columbia* and began the three-day trip home. They brought back about 49 pounds (22 kg) of Moon rocks. They left science experiments, unneeded equipment, an American flag, and a plaque that read, "Here men from the planet Earth first set foot upon the Moon, July 1969 A.D. We came in peace for all mankind."

With Apollo 11's successful Pacific Ocean landing on July 24, 1969, America won the Space Race. But there were many missions yet to come, and much more to be explored.

Astronaut Buzz Aldrin stands by the American flag he and Neil Armstrong planted on the Moon.

CHAPTER 51
APOLLO 12

JUST FOUR MONTHS AFTER APOLLO 11'S HISTORIC MISSION, APOLLO 12 lifted off from Florida's Kennedy Space Center on November 14, 1969. The mission started with some bad luck. As the Saturn V rocket passed through a storm cloud, it was struck by lightning. The spacecraft's electrical systems were knocked out, but backup power quickly came on. All operations were reset, and Apollo 12 was ready to continue.

In three days, astronauts Charles "Pete" Conrad, Alan Bean, and Richard Gordon reached the Moon, nearly a quarter million miles (402,336 km) from Earth.

As Gordon piloted the command module *Yankee Clipper*, Conrad and Bean descended to the Moon in the lunar module *Intrepid*. They made a pinpoint landing on the Ocean of Storms region. (Conrad nicknamed their landing site "Pete's Parking Lot.") After landing, the astronauts were excited to moonwalk. "Those rocks have been waiting four and a half billion years for us to come grab them," said Bean. "Let's go grab a few."

The astronauts performed a pair of four-hour EVAs (extravehicular activities). They collected rock samples, set up science experiments, and measured the Moon's magnetic field. They also took a short hike to Surveyor 3, an American lunar lander that had touched down two years earlier, in 1967. Conrad and Bean took several parts of Surveyor 3 back with them to Earth.

A rare photo of *two* US spacecraft on the Moon. Astronaut Pete Conrad examines Surveyor 3, with the *Intrepid* in the background.

CHAPTER 52
APOLLO 13

On April 11, 1970, Apollo 13 blasted off from NASA's Kennedy Space Center in Florida. With an earthshaking roar, the mighty Saturn V rocket rose into the sky. Five minutes after liftoff, the mission's three astronauts encountered their first problem. The Saturn V's center engine shut down. Luckily, the remaining four engines had enough power to lift them safely into orbit.

The three astronauts inside the command module *Odyssey* were James Lovell, Fred Haise, and John "Jack" Swigert. (Originally, the crew included astronaut Ken Mattingly. However, he was exposed to German measles and was replaced by Swigert three days before launch.) Commander Lovell was a veteran astronaut who flew on Gemini 7, Gemini 12, and Apollo 8. In 1970, he was the most-traveled man in history. Over the course of his previous three missions, he spent 572 days in space covering nearly seven million miles (11.3 million km). Apollo 13 was his chance to finally walk on the Moon.

Apollo 13's other two crew members included command module pilot Jack Swigert and lunar module pilot Fred Haise. Neither had flown in space, but they were both experienced pilots. Each had completed thousands of hours of astronaut training.

Apollo 11 and 12 had explored the Moon's flat plains, called *maria*. Apollo 13's mission was to explore part of the lunar highlands. These tall regions appear brighter to us on Earth. The astronauts were trained to use scientific instruments to study the region's geology.

With the crew nestled safely inside the command module, all seemed to be going well as Apollo 13 sped toward the Moon. Then, just over two days into the mission, the crew heard a loud bang and felt *Odyssey* shudder. Caution and warning lights flashed. Electrical power began to drop. At first, the astronauts thought a meteoroid might have slammed into the spacecraft. Swigert spoke on the radio to NASA's Mission Control in Houston, Texas. "Okay, Houston," he said, "we've had a problem here." Commander Lovell quickly chimed in and confirmed the troubling news.

Unbeknownst to the astronauts or Mission Control, an explosion had ripped through the interior of the service module. The blast was caused by damaged wires on a fan inside an oxygen tank. It contained hundreds of pounds of liquid oxygen, which was used to make breathable air, water, and electricity. Earlier testing by ground technicians accidentally triggered overheating inside the tank, which melted Teflon insulation surrounding the wires.

During Apollo missions, the fan was periodically turned on to stir the liquid oxygen so that level readings were more accurate. Nobody knew about the damage until the fan was turned on 56 hours into the mission. The bare wires short-circuited and sparked a fire. The oxygen-rich tank blew up with the force of a shotgun blast, ripping through wiring, pipes, and valves. One side of the service module was blown outward.

Jim Lovell could see a cloud of gas venting into space from the crippled spacecraft. He knew they were in deep trouble. To make matters worse, they were over 200,000 miles (321,869 km) from Earth, too late to simply turn back.

Despite how the situation was depicted in the 1995 film *Apollo*

13, the astronauts did not argue about who was to blame for the explosion. They remained calm, their only concern the condition of the spacecraft and their own safety.

The blast had knocked out most of the command module's electricity, water, and heat. The crew was forced to shut down electrical systems in the command module. They had to save whatever electricity was left or they wouldn't have sufficient power to safely reenter Earth's atmosphere and land. Lovell, Swigert, and Haise moved into the lunar module *Aquarius* and used it as a lifeboat. Unfortunately, *Aquarius* was built to hold just two people, not three. They barely had enough oxygen, heat, and water to survive the long journey back to Earth.

As Apollo 13 hurtled through space, scientists at Mission Control worked tirelessly. They devised a plan to get the crew home safely without running out of fuel. They informed the astronauts to continue on course and fly once around the Moon. Its gravity would give them a "slingshot" boost back toward Earth.

The spacecraft sped around the Moon at an altitude of about 60 miles (97 km) from the lunar surface, much higher than other Apollo missions. Also, the Moon at the time was at its apogee from Earth during its elliptical orbit. Therefore, Apollo 13 holds the distance record from Earth of a crewed mission, approximately 248,655 miles (400,171 km).

After the slingshot maneuver, the astronauts fired their engine to make mid-course corrections. With help from Mission Control, they were soon on the right path home. But inside the lunar module, the crew's breathing was slowly causing too much carbon dioxide gas to build up in the cabin air. Carbon dioxide is normally expelled when we breathe out. It can quickly accumulate in an enclosed room, such as a spacecraft. Unless it is removed from the air, it builds up in the bloodstream and causes carbon dioxide poisoning, a situation where the brain can't get enough oxygen. This dangerous condition is called hypoxia. It causes confusion, memory loss, and eventually death.

The astronauts ran out of filtration canisters used in a machine that "scrubbed" carbon dioxide out of the foul cabin air. Spare cube-shaped canisters from the command module did not connect with the round hole of the air scrubber in the lunar module. Luckily, Mission Control invented a way for the astronauts to use plastic bags, hoses, a sock, and tape to make the canisters fit.

As the days passed, the crew suffered with little to eat or drink, and with almost no sleep. They also endured freezing temperatures. Finally, they reached Earth on April 17, 1970. They moved back into *Odyssey* and turned the power back on. The crew held their collective breath as they flipped power switches back on. Nobody knew if condensation from the cold might have damaged the command module's electronics. Luckily, everything worked as expected.

Just before reentry, the lunar and service modules were released, and *Odyssey* made a fiery descent through Earth's atmosphere. The crew splashed down safely in the Pacific Ocean, a mere four miles (6.5 km) from the Navy recovery ship USS *Iwo Jima*. The entire world welcomed them home as heroes.

The world cheered as the astronauts returned safely. From left to right: Fred Haise, Jim Lovell, and Jack Swigert.

CHAPTER 53
APOLLO 14

AFTER THE APOLLO 13 DISASTER, SEVERAL CHANGES WERE MADE TO the service module. The oxygen tanks were redesigned to prevent the kind of explosion that crippled the spacecraft. Also, a third tank was added, just in case.

After a four-month delay, Apollo 14 lifted into the sky like crackling thunder on January 31, 1971. Riding atop the Saturn V rocket were astronauts Alan Shepard, the commander of the mission, plus Stuart Roosa and Edgar Mitchell. For Shepard, this flight was a long-awaited comeback. He was one of the original Mercury 7 astronauts, and the first American to fly in space. Medical conditions had kept him grounded for several years, but now he was cleared again for spaceflight. With the Apollo 14 mission, Alan Shepard would become the only Mercury 7 astronaut to walk on the Moon.

The command module on this mission was named *Kitty Hawk*. It would be flown solo by Stuart Roosa during the Moon landing. The lunar module was called *Antares*.

On February 5, 1971, *Antares* began its descent to the Moon with Shepard and Mitchell inside. A computer glitch and a radar malfunction almost caused the mission to abort, but quick thinking by Mission Control and the astronauts saved the day.

Shepard put *Antares* down closer to the landing zone than any other Apollo mission.

Shepard and Mitchell went on two moonwalks, totaling over nine hours. The pair collected 94 pounds (43 kg) of rocks, and conducted several science experiments. Shepard even hit two golf balls with a club he'd brought with him. In the Moon's low gravity, Shepard said the second ball went "Miles and miles and miles."

The crew of Apollo 14 returned to Earth on February 9, 1971, splashing down safely in the Pacific Ocean.

CHAPTER 54
APOLLO 15

ON THE MORNING OF JULY 26, 1971, APOLLO 15 LIFTED OFF FROM the Kennedy Space Center in Florida. The crew included astronauts David Scott, James Irwin, and Al Worden. Soon, they were on their way to the Moon. The command module on this mission was named *Endeavor*. The lunar module was called *Falcon*.

On July 30, after orbiting the Moon several times, Commander Scott and lunar module pilot Irwin began their descent in *Falcon*. Command module pilot Worden flew solo in *Endeavor* while taking high-resolution photos of the surface below.

Falcon landed on the foothills of the Montes Apenninus region (named after the Apennine Mountains in Italy). The mountains rose an average of 15,000 feet (4,572 m) above the lunar plain, about the height of Colorado's Mount Evans.

Over three days, during three moonwalks totaling 18.5 hours, Scott and Irwin collected Moon rocks and performed many science experiments. They also used a new piece of equipment: the lunar roving vehicle (LRV), a battery-powered cart that moved about eight miles per hour (13 kph). It carried the astronauts to distant landmarks and transported heavy loads of rocks and equipment. Assisted by the rover, Scott and Irwin traveled 17.5 miles (28 km) on the surface, far surpassing Apollo 14's record of 2.1 miles (3.4 km).

During the trip back to Earth, Al Worden completed the first spacewalk in deep space. He was sent outside the capsule to retrieve film for a science experiment attached to the spacecraft's hull. *Endeavor* safely splashed down in the Pacific Ocean on August 7, 1971.

Astronaut James Irwin salutes the United States flag at the *Falcon* landing site in the foothills of the Moon's Montes Apenninus region.

CHAPTER 55
APOLLO 16

On April 19, 1972, Apollo 16's command module *Casper* slipped into orbit around the Moon. The next day, Commander John Young and astronaut Charles Duke climbed into the lunar module *Orion* and undocked. Astronaut Ken Mattingly stayed behind and flew *Casper* solo as his crewmates began their descent.

Orion landed in the Descartes Highlands region. It was the first Apollo mission in that part of the Moon. NASA wanted to sample rocks from the area. Geologists were interested to see if there were differences from specimens retrieved by earlier missions.

Young and Duke spent 71 hours on the surface. They took three moonwalks totaling about 20 hours. During that time, they collected 209 pounds (95 kg) of rock samples. They drove their rover almost 17 miles (27 km) across the gray lunar landscape.

Astronaut John Young gives the lunar rover a speed workout at Apollo 16's Descartes Highlands landing site.

In addition to collecting rocks, the astronauts conducted science experiments, including measuring the Moon's magnetic field. They also explored several deep craters and took hundreds of photographs.

On April 24, Young and Duke loaded their rock samples into *Orion*. They strapped themselves in and lifted off in the lunar module's ascent stage. Once in orbit, they docked with *Casper* and transferred their equipment to the command module. Next, they prepared for the journey back to Earth.

On April 27, 1972, the astronauts safely splashed down in the Pacific Ocean. They were picked up by rescue crews from the Navy aircraft carrier USS *Ticonderoga* about 37 minutes after splashdown.

CHAPTER 56
APOLLO 17

APOLLO 17 WAS THE FINAL FLIGHT OF NASA'S APOLLO MISSIONS. Riding inside the command module *America* were astronauts Gene Cernan, Ronald Evans, and Harrison "Jack" Schmitt. Their Saturn V rocket lifted off on the night of December 7, 1972. When the Saturn V's engines ignited, an orange fireball lit up the sky as Apollo 17 sped away from Earth.

On December 11, Cernan and Schmitt descended to the Moon in the lunar module *Challenger*. After a smooth landing on the Moon's Taurus-Littrow region, they went on three moonwalks over three days, collecting 243 pounds (110 kg) of rock samples. They also took photographs of the area, performed science experiments, and explored the boulder-strewn landscape.

Finally, it was time to go home. Commander Gene Cernan was the last Apollo astronaut to depart from the Moon. Before he entered *Challenger*, he took one last look at the desolate, beautiful, alien world. He radioed Mission Control: "As I take man's last step from the surface… for some time to come—but we believe not too long into the future—I'd like to just say what I believe history will record. That America's challenge of today has forged man's destiny of tomorrow. And, as we leave the Moon at Taurus-Littrow, we leave as we came and, God willing, as we shall return, with peace and hope for all mankind. Godspeed the crew of Apollo 17."

Cernan, Evans, and Schmitt safely splashed down in the Pacific Ocean on December 19, 1972. Project Apollo had come to a spectacular end.

Harrison Schmitt plants an American flag in the lunar soil, with the Earth shining in the background.

SPACE STATIONS AND BEYOND

CHAPTER 57
BEYOND THE SPACE RACE

On July 20, 1969, astronaut Neil Armstrong, commander of the American Apollo 11 mission, stepped on the Moon. At that moment, the Space Race came to an unofficial end.

During the 1950s and 1960s, the United States and the Soviet Union invested much effort in the race to the Moon. Billions of dollars were spent. Lives were lost. The winner could claim national honor and prestige. Also at stake: learning how to lob bigger and more destructive bombs at each other's cities. The Space Race, after all, received funding or support from each country's military, especially in the early days.

More Moon missions followed Apollo 11. However, public support for manned spaceflight shrank. Planners in both countries started thinking about the future. What kind of spacecraft should be built next? The answer: space stations.

A space station is a spacecraft that stays in orbit around Earth for a long time, sometimes for many years. It is usually occupied by a crew. Some Russian cosmonauts have spent more than a year at a time aboard a space station. (Several cosmonauts and astronauts have spent time on multiple trips totaling more than one year.)

For more than a century, people have dreamed of living in

space. There are many tales of science fiction that take place on space stations. Serious scientists have also pushed for a permanent spacecraft in orbit where astronauts can work.

Space stations can be used in many ways. They often serve as laboratories where unique medicines and materials are produced, thanks to the weightless environment.

Space stations can also be used to observe Earth, including its landforms and weather. In addition, telescopes and other instruments get clearer views of the planets and stars, since space stations are so high up they are free from Earth's thick, light-obscuring atmosphere.

Besides science experiments, space stations are excellent places for astronauts to train, possibly for long-duration trips to Mars or other planets. The lessons learned by working in space for long periods of time help scientists develop new technology for future spaceflights.

During the competitive years of the Space Race, both the United States and the Soviet Union learned the basics of building space stations that could orbit Earth. The Soviets—later the Russians, after the collapse of the Soviet Union in 1991—had a head start. Russian cosmonauts have been in space almost continuously since 1971.

Once the Apollo program was finished in the early 1970s, the United States considered building large space stations. But they were considered too expensive and complicated. Instead, the National Aeronautics and Space Administration (NASA) spent most of its efforts building a fleet of space shuttles, which were sent into orbit frequently but for shorter durations.

Eventually, the two Space Race competitors, the United States and the Russian Federation, agreed to cooperate. They combined their knowledge and built a large space station, together with several other nations. So far, the International Space Station (ISS) has been the most successful space station in history.

The American space shuttle *Atlantis* and the Russian Mir space station photographed from a Soyuz spacecraft on July 4, 1995. In the years following the Space Race, joint Russian and American activities helped advance the scientific knowledge of both countries.

CHAPTER 58
SALYUT SPACE STATIONS

THE WORLD'S FIRST SPACE STATION, SALYUT 1, WAS LAUNCHED INTO orbit on April 19, 1971, from the Soviet Union's Baikonur Cosmodrome in Kazakhstan. This was a time when America was still sending manned Apollo missions to the Moon.

The Soviets had little hope of equaling the American achievement. Instead, they decided to put more effort into building a permanent presence in space. Salyut 1 was the first in a series of Salyut space stations. (In Russian, the word Salyut means "salute.") Over the next 10 years, six more Salyuts followed. Even though seven Salyuts reached orbit, only six were successfully crewed. (Salyut 2 failed after two days.)

All Salyuts were launched into space in one piece by Proton rockets. Once in orbit, they were powered by two sets of solar panels that jutted outward like wings. Salyut 1 was shaped like a big cylinder, about 66 feet long (20 m) and 13 feet (4 m) in diameter. Future Salyuts were slightly bigger.

The Salyut program was active for about 15 years, until 1986. More than 70 cosmonauts worked on Salyuts for a total of 1,696 days. They entered and left the space stations through a docking port on the end. The cosmonauts conducted experiments and noted how weightlessness affects the human body. Some also carried out secret military tests. When the Salyut missions were finished, the space stations were allowed to burn up in Earth's atmosphere.

The Russian Salyut 6 space station. Two Soyuz spacecraft are docked on the left and right ends of the station.

CHAPTER 59
SOYUZ SPACECRAFT

TO FERRY COSMONAUTS AND SUPPLIES TO AND FROM SPACE STATIONS, the Russian space program uses Soyuz spacecraft. (Soyuz means "union.") They have been workhorses since their introduction in 1967 by the Soviet Union for its Moon program. The spacecraft design has been improved over the years. They are now extremely reliable, and are still flying today to the International Space Station (ISS). They have been used longer than any other manned spacecraft.

Modern Soyuz capsules can carry three cosmonauts, plus food, water, and other supplies. They are launched atop large rockets, which are also called Soyuz. The spacecraft have three parts, including orbital, descent, and service modules. The middle, bell-shaped descent module is the section that returns to Earth.

A Soyuz is always docked to the ISS. It can act as a lifeboat and emergency escape vehicle in case a catastrophe requires that the space station be evacuated.

Soyuz spacecraft land on the flat, grassy plains of Kazakhstan. (They land on the ground because Russia does not keep a large navy at sea at all times to perform rescues.) During reentry, Earth's thick atmosphere slows the spacecraft down. Large parachutes further slow its descent. At the last moment, four retro-rockets fire, and the Soyuz lands with a thump. Rescue crews are almost immediately at the scene to extract the cosmonauts.

CHAPTER 60
SOYUZ 11 TRAGEDY

SALYUT 1, THE SOVIET UNION'S FIRST SPACE STATION, LIFTED OFF ON April 19, 1971. When it went into orbit, it did not yet have a crew. Two days later, the Soyuz 10 spacecraft with three cosmonauts aboard blasted off from the Baikonur Cosmodrome on the grassy plains of Kazakhstan. Their mission was expected to last 30 days, but when they rendezvoused with the space station, they could not get their spacecraft's docking hatch to open to let them inside. The mission was canceled, and they returned to Earth.

On June 6, the Soviets tried again with Soyuz 11 and a fresh batch of cosmonauts: Georgi Dobrovolski, Vladislav Volkov, and Viktor Patsayev. They successfully docked with Salyut 1 and were able to enter, the first time in history a space station had held a crew. They settled in for a three-week mission that included 383 orbits around Earth, setting a record for the longest time in space.

On June 29, the cosmonauts prepared to go home. They reentered their spacecraft, but because the capsule was so cramped, they did not wear spacesuits. After undocking, they fired their retrorockets and began the long descent to Earth.

Soyuz 11 seemed to reenter the atmosphere and land normally. Despite controllers being unable to raise the crew on the radio, all systems appeared to be fine. But when the recovery team opened the capsule, they found all three cosmonauts dead inside, still strapped to their seats.

After an investigation, the Soviets discovered that a ventilation valve had accidentally opened on the Soyuz spacecraft, decompressing the cabin. The loss of air killed the cosmonauts within minutes. To this day, they are the only three people known to have died in space.

Dobrovolski, Volkov, and Patsayev were hailed as national heroes of the Soviet Union and given state funerals. Afterwards, the Soyuz capsule was modified to only hold two people, which gave the cosmonauts room to wear spacesuits. Soyuz was eventually redesigned and made bigger, allowing a crew of three to wear lightweight spacesuits.

The Salyut 1 space station was never used again. On October 11, 1971, orders were given for it to be deorbited. It later broke apart over the Pacific Ocean.

CHAPTER 61
SKYLAB

THE UNITED STATES' FIRST SPACE STATION WAS CALLED SKYLAB. IT was a short-term science laboratory where crews performed experiments in the weightlessness of low Earth orbit.

Skylab was launched on May 14, 1973, a little more than two years after the Soviet Union's Salyut 1 space station. It was boosted into orbit atop a Saturn V rocket, modified so that its third stage became an orbiting laboratory. Three different crews—nine astronauts in total—worked in Skylab.

After the Apollo 11 mission to the Moon, NASA made recommendations for future space operations to President Richard Nixon once all the Apollo flights were completed. The agency's ambitious plan included a permanently manned space station. It wanted a fleet of space shuttles to ferry crews and supplies back and forth. Eventually, NASA also wanted to send manned missions to Mars.

Because the United States economy was not doing well, only the space shuttle program received full government funding. However, after the last two Apollo missions were canceled, NASA used one of the remaining Saturn V rockets to make Skylab affordable. It wished to prove to the American people that astronauts could live and work in space for long periods of time, and conduct valuable science research.

When Skylab launched in May 1973, it immediately had problems. A micrometeoroid shield tore away and destroyed a solar panel. It also caused another to stick. The accident meant Skylab had less power than planned. It also caused overheating from the Sun without the shield in place.

Skylab's first crew saved the station by performing several spacewalks. They managed to replace the shield and unjam the stubborn solar panel. Temperatures in Skylab slowly dropped to near-normal levels, and the crew was able to work safely inside. The spacewalks and repairs proved the value of having a human crew on future space missions.

Skylab was about 82 feet (25 m) long and 22 feet (7 m) in diameter. It had four major parts. They included an airlock, a docking module, an orbital workshop, and a telescope mount. A solar telescope gave the astronauts opportunities to take pictures of sun flares.

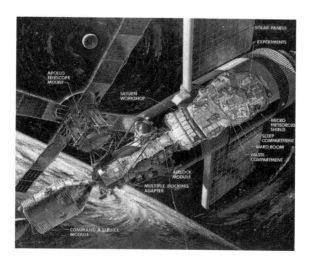

The orbital workshop is where the astronauts worked and slept. NASA tried to make it as comfortable as possible. It had the same amount of room as a small house. It included exercise equipment, private sleeping quarters, a shower, and windows to view Earth.

Skylab was occupied by three different crews from May 25, 1973, until February 8, 1974. Combined, they performed 270 science experiments in astronomy, physics, and biology. They traveled more than 70 million miles (113 million km) over 171 days in orbit.

When the Skylab program ended, the space station reentered Earth's atmosphere in July 1979. Most of Skylab burned up, but some pieces fell to the ground in western Australia. Nobody was injured.

CHAPTER 62
APOLLO-SOYUZ TEST PROJECT

IN 1972, THE UNITED STATES AND THE SOVIET UNION AGREED TO FLY a space mission together. Three years later, the agreement became reality when the Apollo-Soyuz Test Project launched.

On July 15, 1975, two spacecraft lifted off from opposite sides of the world. A Soviet Soyuz spacecraft carrying a pair of cosmonauts launched from the Baikonur Cosmodrome in Kazakhstan. A few hours later, three American astronauts atop a Saturn 1B rocket lifted off from the Kennedy Space Center in Florida. Two days later, the two capsules rendezvoused and docked. It was a mission that seemed impossible just a few years earlier.

The Apollo-Soyuz Test Project was the first time that the Space Race rivals worked together on a manned flight. Much work was yet to be done, but the mission was the start of a partnership that eventually saw the construction of the largest space station in history.

Apollo-Soyuz was designed to prove how well Soviet and American spacecraft could dock with each other. The countries realized that in case of a space station emergency, it would be a tremendous advantage if either side could help the other. But in order for an international rescue mission to work, the docking hardware on all spacecraft had to fit together.

Engineers from the Soviet Union and the United States shared their data and experience. They designed a new docking module that fit both the American Apollo spacecraft and the Soviet Soyuz capsule.

The two Soviet cosmonauts on the mission were Alexey Leonov and Valery Kubasov. Leonov was the first person to ever spacewalk. He made history during his Voskhod 2 mission in 1965.

The three American astronauts included Thomas Stafford, Donald "Deke" Slayton, and Vance Brand. Slayton was one of the original Mercury 7 astronauts. He had been grounded because of an irregular heartbeat. The condition had cleared, and Slayton now finally had his chance to go into space.

The two spacecraft rendezvoused on July 17, 1975. They inched closer together, and then the astronauts felt a slight jolt. They had docked. Soon, the hatches on each capsule opened and commanders Stafford and Leonov shook hands. "Glad to see you," Stafford said in Russian. Leonov smiled and replied in English, "Glad to see you. Very, very happy to see you."

Over the next two days, the astronauts and cosmonauts visited each other's spacecraft and conducted science experiments. They ate meals together and exchanged gifts.

People in both the United States and the Soviet Union were relieved when the joint spaceflight happened. It seemed as if the Cold War was finally thawing. Perhaps the future held more cooperation between the superpowers instead of the constant threat of conflict.

CHAPTER 63
SPACE SHUTTLE

NASA's space shuttle was the world's first reusable spacecraft. It took off like a rocket, but landed like a glider. It carried heavy payloads, such as satellites and science labs, and brought them back to Earth for repair when needed.

The space shuttle was meant to be a cheaper alternative to expensive single-use rockets. It could safely land, be refurbished and refueled, and be ready to launch again in just a few weeks.

The shuttle had many purposes. It ferried astronauts to and from the International Space Station (ISS), and it launched probes and observatories like the Hubble Space Telescope. It was also used to conduct scientific research during orbital trips that lasted from one to two weeks. One of its most important jobs was to transport large sections of the ISS into orbit.

Officially called the Space Transportation System, when fully prepared for a vertical launch the spacecraft was comprised of three main parts: The orbiter held the crew (usually up to seven astronauts), plus any payload inside its cavernous rear cargo hold. The orbiter measured 122 feet (37 m) long, with a wingspan of 78 feet (24 m). Once in space, the shuttle orbited the Earth at about 17,500 miles per hour (28,164 kph), circling the planet approximately every 45 minutes.

Attached to the orbiter at launch was a rust-colored external tank. It supplied 500,000 gallons (1.9 million liters) of liquid oxygen and liquid hydrogen fuel to the orbiter's three main engines. When it ran out of fuel, it ejected from the orbiter. Most of the external tank burned up as it fell through the atmosphere.

A pair of solid-rocket boosters were attached to either side of the external tank. They provided most of the thrust during liftoff. When their fuel supply was exhausted, they dropped off and parachuted into the Atlantic Ocean, where they were picked up, refurbished, and used again by later shuttle flights.

The space shuttle was the size of a modern jetliner and shaped like an aerodynamic wing (called a delta wing). Its shape allowed it to return to Earth like a glider. Special heat-resistant tiles on its lower half kept it from burning up when reentering the atmosphere. When it descended close to the ground, it lowered its wheels and landed on a runway like an airplane (except for a large parachute it released to help it slow down).

NASA built five fully functioning space shuttle orbiters. They were named *Atlantis, Challenger, Columbia, Discovery,* and *Endeavour*. The first space shuttle flight was in 1981. The last flight occurred in 2011. During this period, there were 135 missions. All flights launched from the Kennedy Space Center in Florida.

SPACE SHUTTLE

Space shuttle *Atlantis* soared into space with a crew of seven and a payload of scientific equipment destined for the International Space Station in 1992. NASA's space shuttles were used repeatedly from the first shuttle flight in 1981 until the fleet was retired in 2011. After 135 shuttle missions spanning more than 30 years, *Atlantis* made the final flight in July 2011.

CHAPTER 64
THE CHALLENGER AND COLUMBIA TRAGEDIES

By 1986, space shuttle flights were so common they seemed routine. NASA appeared to have perfected spaceflight. On January 28, 1986, that thought was proven tragically wrong.

The space shuttle *Challenger* was starting its 10th mission. Less than two minutes after liftoff, there was a massive explosion in the sky. All seven astronauts were killed. The crew included Commander Francis Scobee, pilot Michael Smith, Ellison Onizuka, Judith Resnik, Ronald McNair, Christa McAuliffe, and Gregory Jarvis. McAuliffe was part of the Teacher in Space program.

NASA later determined that a faulty rubber O-ring seal on one of the solid rocket boosters had hardened because of cold weather. That allowed burning gas to leak like a blowtorch. The flames struck the neighboring external liquid-fuel tank, causing it to explode.

In 2003, tragedy again struck the space shuttle program. On February 1, 2003, in the final minutes of its mission, *Columbia* broke apart over the skies of Texas. During reentry, a broken heat shield panel on the left wing allowed hot gasses to enter. That led to the shuttle's destruction and the deaths of the entire crew of seven astronauts. They included Commander Rick Husband, pilot

William McCool, Kalpana Chawla, David Brown, Laurel Clark, Ilan Ramon, and Michael Anderson.

The *Challenger* and *Columbia* disasters brought about changes in space shuttle design to make them safer. NASA also made much-needed reforms in management. The accidents reminded people that, far from being routine, there is always danger when venturing into space.

CHAPTER 65
MIR SPACE STATION

AFTER THE SUCCESS OF THE SOVIET UNION'S SALYUT SPACE STATIONS, the Soviets began building a bigger station that could be inhabited for much longer periods of time. They named it Mir, which means "world," or "peace," in Russian.

Mir was the first modular space station. It was built over time using several large pieces assembled together. The first piece was launched into orbit by a Soviet Proton rocket in 1986. The module had six docking ports for future sections or for visiting spacecraft. Construction on Mir continued until 1996. By then, it had become the largest space station ever built. Mir stayed in orbit for 15 years. That was three times longer than expected. It even lasted longer than the Soviet Union. In 1991, control of Mir was transferred to the Russian Federation and its new space agency.

When it was completed, Mir had the appearance of a Tinkertoy in space. Many modules jutted out at strange angles. The central module served as a living quarters for the crew. It was a large metal cylinder about 43 feet (13 m) long and 14 feet (4 m) in diameter. Electricity came from solar panels that jutted out of the module like wings.

Other modules were added over the next decade. They included an observatory, science labs, and an additional life-support module. Most of the cosmonauts traveled to and from the space station by Soyuz spacecraft. Supplies were sent by unmanned Progress cargo spacecraft.

Despite its appearance, the station was a success. It proved that people could live in orbit for months at a time. Mir was a science laboratory in space. Besides testing human biology in a weightless environment, the station's crews performed many experiments in botany, physics, astronomy, and biomedicine. They also learned valuable knowledge about spacecraft systems.

Mir had 28 different crews during its lifetime. Each mission lasted about six months, but some cosmonauts stayed longer. Valery Polyakov set a space endurance record between January 1994 and March 1995. He lived on the space station for 438 days in a row. Mir's crews were mostly Russian cosmonauts, but the space station also hosted dozens of guests from countries all over the world.

Starting in the mid-1990s, American space shuttles began docking with Mir. American astronauts and equipment were also delivered. The space shuttle-Mir missions were part of a new cooperation between the space programs of the United States and Russia. The lessons learned would later be used to construct the most ambitious spacecraft in history: the International Space Station.

In March 2001, the Russian space agency used retrorockets on the aging Mir to bring it down to Earth. The deorbit happened over the Pacific Ocean. Most of Mir burned up, but some flaming debris splashed into the ocean.

CHAPTER 66
INTERNATIONAL SPACE STATION

THE FIERCE SPACE RACE COMPETITION BETWEEN THE SOVIET UNION—later Russia—and the United States eventually led to cooperation between the superpower rivals. Each side concluded that it was best to combine their knowledge—and money—to construct a new space station that would be superior to anything they could make alone. In fact, their plans were so ambitious that many other countries also joined the effort and provided their own expertise. The result is the International Space Station (ISS), the most advanced space exploration project undertaken to date.

The ISS has been continuously crewed since November 2000. It is a modular space station, like Mir, with large sections added from time to time as needed. The station orbits an average of 260 miles (418 km) above Earth, taking about 90 minutes to complete one trip around the planet. That means the astronauts aboard can witness 16 sunrises and 16 sunsets during each 24-hour day.

Today, the ISS is an orbiting science laboratory. Its occupants are learning the best ways to live and work in space. This information will help future astronauts explore distant places in our solar system, perhaps even Mars.

Construction of the ISS took years to plan and the help of 15 nations. The station's five principal partners include NASA and space agencies from Russia, Europe, Canada, and Japan. Russia launched the first piece of the ISS, called Zarya, into orbit in 1998. A few weeks later, an American module named Unity was connected, transported into low-Earth orbit by the space shuttle *Endeavour*. More than a dozen pressurized modules plus major equipment upgrades have been added in the years since, brought to the ISS by Russian rockets, NASA's fleet of space shuttles, and rockets from private industry, including Northrop Grumman, Lockheed Martin, and SpaceX. Other companies that will soon join the effort to service the ISS include Boeing, Sierra Space, and Axiom Space. As of January 2022, there are 16 pressurized modules in which astronauts live and work, slightly larger in volume than an average five-bedroom home.

The International Space Station's solar arrays provide power for the orbiting laboratory.

NASA has three primary goals for the ISS: It is a place for astronauts to conduct scientific research in a weightless environment. It establishes a constant, long-term presence in space. It also encourages many countries to work together. To date, over 2,800 science experiments have been conducted on the ISS so far.

Fully crewed, the ISS can support six astronauts, although

during crew swaps it can temporarily handle more. The first long-term crew to live aboard the ISS arrived in 2000. They included Sergei Krikalev and Yuri Gidzenko from Russia, plus William Shepherd of the United States. Astronauts and cosmonauts have occupied the ISS ever since that date.

Over its lifetime, crews from many nations have lived and worked on the ISS. They have added additional living quarters, science laboratories, solar panels, and communications systems. The ISS today is slightly bigger in area than an American football field. If one could put it on a scale on Earth, it would weigh over 925,000 pounds (419,573 kg).

Most of the space station's bulk is in its cylinder- or sphere-shaped modules. They are linked and pressurized so astronauts can live and work inside. Some are the size of small rooms, while others are as big as a city bus.

Besides living quarters, ISS modules contain life-support equipment that supplies air and water for the crew. Other modules contain navigation equipment, electrical components, or science experiments. Special modules have docking ports for visiting spacecraft, or airlocks so astronauts using spacesuits can venture out to work on the station's exterior. Up to eight spacecraft can be docked to the ISS at once.

One special module is the dome-shaped Cupola. Built in Italy, it has large windows that give astronauts a panoramic view of the space station and the Earth. The windows are useful when astronauts use the ISS's Canadarm2 robotic arm system. Made in Canada, it is used to assemble and repair the outside of ISS modules. It can also capture and dock unmanned supply spacecraft that visit the ISS.

The ISS gets its electrical power from large solar arrays. They are made of thousands of solar cells that absorb energy from the Sun and convert it into electricity. The solar arrays are arranged in four pairs on each side of the space station. Each array is about 240 feet (73 m) long, which is longer than the wingspan of a Boeing 777 airliner. When the ISS moves into Earth's shadow during its 90-minute orbit, the space station gets its power from rechargeable batteries.

Astronauts and cosmonauts from 19 different countries have served aboard the ISS. There are usually three to six people living there at once. Space station missions are called expeditions. Each usually lasts about six months.

Living on the ISS is much more comfortable than earlier space station expeditions. Astronauts sleep inside their own closet-sized cubbies. Sleeping bags provide warmth and keep them from floating away. After waking, they wash with moist towels. There are no showers because water bubbles might float into electronic equipment and cause damage.

Most food aboard the ISS is dehydrated to save space. Water is first added before eating. Drinking water comes in a package with a straw on the end.

Exercise is important so that astronauts don't lose too much bone density and muscle mass while in orbit. They stay in shape by using a treadmill, stationary bike, and weight-lifting machine at least two hours a day.

The ISS toilet is a small booth. Crew members pee into a vacuum tube that whisks away urine. Feces is disposed of by sitting on a small metal seat with a hole on top. A vacuum sucks away any solid waste. Accidental messes are cleaned up with disinfectant wipes.

Astronauts stay very busy on the ISS maintaining the station and conducting science experiments. Many investigations involving chemistry, physics, and biology can only be carried out in the weightlessness of space. The Japanese Kibo space laboratory is the single largest module on the ISS. It is used to conduct research in astronomy, biology, and space medicine. It is possible that someday many medicines and special materials will be manufactured in space, thanks to the work done on the ISS. There are even future plans to grow human hearts and other organs in space.

Eventually, the ISS will be too old to maintain and will have to be replaced. For now, NASA expects it to operate at least through the 2020s and possibly a decade or two beyond. In December 2021, the Biden-Harris Administration committed to extend the station's operations through 2030, and to work with America's international partners to continue their groundbreaking scientific studies. That includes working with instruments that directly help us on Earth, such as measuring the effects of climate change, drought, and forest health.

When the International Space Station someday reaches its end of operations, it will be remotely steered out of its orbit and brought down by gravity somewhere in a remote part of the South Pacific Ocean. Most of it will burn up in Earth's atmosphere, although some large pieces of debris may survive and splash into the sea.

It is possible that the International Space Station will not meet such a fiery end. As we will see in the following chapter, many countries and private companies have plans to construct their own space stations in the near future. They may decide to purchase or lease sections of the ISS for their own use. If major parts of the ISS are recycled in this way, they may yet circle the Earth for many decades to come.

CHAPTER 67
FUTURE SPACE STATIONS

THE INTERNATIONAL SPACE STATION IS NOT THE ONLY STATION currently in orbit around Earth. In 2011, China launched a small space station called Tiangong-1. It was followed by Tiangong-2 in 2016. Tiangong-1's orbit eventually decayed, probably burning up in Earth's atmosphere in early 2018. Tiangong-2 was deorbited in July 2019. With the experience learned from these two stations, China began construction of its first long-term crewed space station, dubbed Tiangong ("Palace in the Sky"), the same name as its predecessors but without the number.

The first core module of Tiangong was launched into orbit on April 29, 2021. Two additional modules are planned for 2022. When complete, the station will be about one-fifth of the mass of the ISS, about the size of the old Russian Mir space station. It has a planned lifespan of 10 years, possibly extended to 15 years. Additional modules may be added in the near future.

China plans to conduct science experiments aboard Tiangong and to test docking and transportation systems. It will also host astronauts from other countries, such as Australia and the United Arab Emirates, which want to do scientific research but don't have space stations of their own. For its part, China hopes to learn enough to further its ambitions for future deep space missions, such as crewed expeditions to the Moon or Mars.

Competing for room in low Earth orbit is not limited to the United States and China. A new Russian space station, the Russian Orbital Service Station, is scheduled to begin construction in the mid-2020s. Russia hopes to have a crew aboard by 2026. India has ambitions to launch its own space station by 2030, becoming just the fourth country in the world—behind the United States, Russia, and China—to accomplish such a massive undertaking.

With the ISS set to be retired in less than a decade, NASA is planning for future space station replacements so that the United States can continue having a presence in low Earth orbit. To save money—some estimates go as high as $1 billion annually—the space agency plans to share the high cost of space station construction and operation with private industry.

To foster commercial space stations in partnership with the private sector, NASA is providing funding, brainpower, and astronauts to at least a dozen interested companies. There are several concept stations on the drawing board, including Blue Origin and Sierra Space's ambitious Orbital Reef project. The modular, 10-person station will contain science labs, manufacturing equipment for making products in microgravity, and even a working garden. There will also be opportunities for space tourists to visit. Sierra Space's Dream Chaser spacecraft will transport equipment and crews to and from the space station. Other corporate partners include Boeing, Redwire Space, and Genesis Engineering. If construction goes according to schedule, Orbital Reef will be operating as soon as the second half of the 2020s.

In addition to Orbital Reef, NASA is also partially funding Starlab, a four-astronaut space station being constructed by corporate partners Nanoracks, Voyager Space, and Lockheed Martin. The station could be operational as early as 2027. Besides Starlab, NASA awarded money to a company called Axiom Space, which will build modules that connect to the ISS. Before the ISS is retired and deorbited, Axiom Space could potentially detach its modules and turn them into a separate space station.

Low Earth orbit is not the only place for future space stations. Now that private industry is well on its way to developing Earth-orbiting space stations, NASA is focusing its energy on deep space, starting with Earth's closest neighbor.

NASA's Artemis program aims to establish a long-term human presence on the Moon. Through a series of ambitious missions, Artemis will spur new industries and technologies critical to further space exploration. NASA is partnering with private industry, the European Space Agency (ESA), Japan Aerospace Exploration Agency (JAXA), and the Canadian Space Agency (CSA) to make possible a permanently crewed base on the Moon. (Artemis is named after the Greek goddess Artemis, the daughter of Zeus and Leto, and the twin sister of Apollo.)

A planned part of the new Moon base is an orbiting outpost called Gateway. It is a mini version of the ISS, about one-sixth its size, with room for four astronauts. It is a modular space station that will operate in cislunar space, between Earth and the Moon. Gateway is scheduled to be assembled in the late-2020s by astronauts flying in NASA's new Orion spacecraft and Space Launch System (SLS) rocket. SpaceX's Dragon XL resupply spacecraft and Falcon Heavy rocket will deliver additional payloads.

Gateway can teach scientists the best way for astronauts to live and work in deep space, thousands of times farther from Earth than the ISS. Astronauts aboard Gateway will perform science experiments and possibly control robots on the Moon's surface. The station will be a communication hub between Earth and the Moon base under construction. Moon landers could be used multiple times, shuttling astronauts and supplies to and from the surface base and Gateway. With more supplies available at a previously stocked space station, crewed missions could last longer, up to 60 days, twice the duration of single direct missions from Earth. Gateway could also serve as a safe harbor in case of a catastrophic accident at the Moon base.

Not everyone believes Gateway is necessary to build a Moon base. The cost, they argue, is too high, and the potential science to be learned is meager. NASA, however, is forging ahead with the project, convinced of its advantages. And if all goes well, Gateway may even be used as a supply station to construct future spacecraft that will whisk astronauts to Mars and beyond.

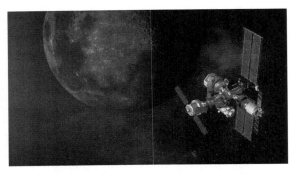

An artist's depiction of the Gateway space station orbiting the Moon.

ASTRONAUTS AND COSMONAUTS

CHAPTER 68
BUZZ ALDRIN

Edwin "Buzz" Aldrin (b. 1930) is a former NASA astronaut, United States Air Force jet pilot, and engineer. He was the pilot of the Apollo 11 lunar module *Eagle*. On July 20, 1969, he became the second person to walk on the Moon, just a few minutes after mission commander Neil Armstrong. Before the Apollo 11 mission, Aldrin first went into space in 1966, piloting the Gemini 12 spacecraft. He performed three spacewalks totaling 5 hours and 30 minutes, which was a record at the time.

Born Edwin E. Aldrin on January 20, 1930, in Montclair, New Jersey, he was known by his nickname, "Buzz." His father was an aviation pioneer who took Buzz on his first plane ride at age two.

Growing up in New Jersey, Buzz had a passion for football and hated schoolwork. With his father's help, he eventually became more serious about his studies. He attended the United States Military Academy at West Point, New York. After graduation, he joined the United States Air Force in 1951. During the Korean War, he flew 66 combat missions in F-86 jet fighters. After the war,

Aldrin earned a Ph.D. in astronautics from the Massachusetts Institute of Technology.

In 1963, Aldrin became part of the third group of astronauts selected by NASA to train for missions in space. With his engineering and astronautics knowledge, he helped develop tools and skills needed to spacewalk, dock spacecraft, and land safely on the Moon.

After his NASA career, Aldrin became the commander of the United States Air Force Test Pilot School at California's Edwards Air Force Base. He retired in 1972, becoming an author and promoter of space exploration.

CHAPTER 69
NEIL ARMSTRONG

Neil Armstrong (1930–2012) commanded the Apollo 11 NASA Moon mission. Traveling with Armstrong were fellow astronauts Edwin "Buzz" Aldrin and Michael Collins. On July 20, 1969, Armstrong descended to the Moon along with Aldrin in the *Eagle* lunar module. They were aiming for a smooth region called the Sea of Tranquility.

As the *Eagle* dropped closer to the Moon, Armstrong became alarmed. The landing site was strewn with boulders big enough to destroy their spacecraft. Armstrong relied on all his past skills as an astronaut, naval aviator, and test pilot. Always cool under pressure, he took over manual control of the *Eagle* and expertly flew it to a safer area. With their fuel levels critically low, the spaceship finally touched down gently on the Moon's surface. "Houston," Armstrong radioed back to Earth, "Tranquility Base here. The *Eagle* has landed."

Neil A. Armstrong was born on his grandparents' farm on August 5, 1930, near the small town of Wapakoneta, Ohio. His father took him on an airplane ride when he was six years old. That was when he knew he wanted to be a pilot. Armstrong earned his pilot license by age 16, even before he had a driver's license. He also became an Eagle Scout in the Boy Scouts of America.

Armstrong studied aeronautical engineering for two years at Indiana's Purdue University before becoming a Navy pilot in 1949. At age 20, he was the youngest pilot in his squadron. He flew 78 combat missions during the Korean War.

After his military career, Armstrong finished his college degree and then became a civilian test pilot. He worked for a government group called the National Advisory Committee for Aeronautics (NACA). In 1958, it became part of the National Aeronautics and Space Administration (NASA). Armstrong flew more than 200 different aircraft, including the X-15 rocket plane. It was a record-setting aircraft that flew very high at over 4,500 miles per hour (7,242 kph).

During his years as a test pilot, Armstrong developed a reputation for quick thinking under stress. He calmly used his scientific knowledge and strong instincts to get himself out of dangerous situations. In 1962, NASA chose him as part of their second group of astronauts. He commanded the Gemini 8 mission in 1966, flying into space with astronaut David Scott. They were the first astronauts to dock two vehicles together in orbit.

Armstrong's second trip to space came in 1969, when he commanded the Apollo 11 mission. After skillfully piloting the lunar module *Eagle* to the surface, he became the first person to set foot on the Moon. He radioed to Earth, "That's one small step for a man, one giant leap for mankind."

Armstrong retired from NASA shortly after the Apollo 11 mission. He became a college professor and a businessman. He hated bragging about his achievements in space, preferring instead to thank the thousands of men and women at NASA who helped make his moonwalk possible. Neil Armstrong died on August 25, 2012, from complications he suffered after heart surgery. He was 82.

CHAPTER 70
GUY BLUFORD

Guion "Guy" Bluford (b. 1942) is the first African American to fly in space. He was a mission specialist on four space shuttle missions. His first was in August 1983 aboard the space shuttle *Challenger*. He and the other four astronauts aboard released a communications satellite and tested the remote Canadarm robotic arm system. Bluford also flew on space shuttle missions in 1985, 1991, and 1992. In total, he logged more than 688 hours in orbit around the Earth.

Bluford was born in Philadelphia, Pennsylvania. He was very interested in science in school. He eventually earned a doctorate degree in aerospace engineering.

Bluford became a US Air Force pilot in 1966. He flew 144 combat missions during the Vietnam War. He was also a flight instructor. Bluford logged more than 5,200 hours of jet flying time.

After retiring from NASA in 1993, Bluford worked for several aerospace companies.

CHAPTER 71
FRANK BORMAN

FRANK BORMAN (B. 1928) COMMANDED Apollo 8, the first manned mission to travel around the Moon. Together with Jim Lovell and Bill Anders, the astronauts blasted off in their Apollo spacecraft on December 21, 1968. It was a dangerous journey that set the stage for later Moon landings. After six days, including 10 orbits around the Moon, the crew returned safely to Earth.

Borman was born in Gary, Indiana, but his family later moved to Tucson, Arizona, where he learned to fly at age 15. After becoming a test pilot for the US Air Force, Borman joined NASA in 1962.

In 1965, Borman commanded Gemini 7, flying along with astronaut Jim Lovell. They set an endurance record of 14 days.

On Christmas Eve, December 24, 1968, as Apollo 8 orbited the Moon, Borman sent this message back home: "And from the crew of Apollo 8, we close with good night, good luck, a Merry Christmas and God bless all of you—all of you on the good Earth."

CHAPTER 72
SCOTT CARPENTER

Scott Carpenter (1925–2013) was the second American to orbit the Earth. His Mercury space capsule, which he named *Aurora 7*, was hurled into space atop an Atlas rocket on May 24, 1962. It was the fourth flight of the Mercury program. Carpenter orbited the Earth three times in a flight lasting nearly five hours.

Carpenter was born in Boulder, Colorado. He was a US Navy jet pilot and flew missions during the Korean War. He later became a test pilot, and was chosen by NASA in 1959 to become one of the original Mercury 7 astronauts. During his flight in *Aurora 7*, he became the first person to eat food in space. He also performed several science experiments while in orbit.

In 1963, Carpenter joined the Navy's SEALAB project. He spent 30 days in 1965 living in a habitat on the ocean floor. He later used his skills to help astronauts train underwater for space-walking missions.

CHAPTER 73
GENE CERNAN

As the commander of Apollo 17 in December 1972, astronaut Eugene "Gene" Cernan (1934–2017) was the last person to walk on the Moon. He was also one of the few astronauts to travel to the Moon twice. On the Apollo 10 mission in May 1969, Cernan was the lunar module pilot. This rehearsal mission tested all the Apollo systems and hardware, but didn't actually land.

Cernan was born in Chicago, Illinois. After earning a college degree in electrical engineering, he joined the US Navy and learned to fly jet fighters. He was chosen by NASA to become an astronaut in 1963. His first space mission was as the pilot of Gemini 9A. He also performed a two-hour spacewalk.

Cernan finally made it to the lunar surface during the Apollo 17 mission. As command module pilot Ronald Evans orbited high above, Cernan and fellow astronaut Harrison Schmitt collected rock samples and conducted science experiments. They spent more than three days on the Moon, a record that stands to this day.

CHAPTER 74
LEROY CHIAO

Leroy Chiao (b. 1960) was selected in 1990 by NASA to become an astronaut. He eventually had a 15-year career with the space agency. He has flown into space four times. He was a mission specialist on three space shuttle flights. He also commanded the International Space Station (ISS) from October 2004 to April 2005. He was the first Asian American to command the ISS. In total, he logged more than 229 days in space.

Chiao was born in Milwaukee, Wisconsin, but grew up in Danville, California. Both of his parents were immigrants from the Republic of China (Taiwan). He is a native English speaker, but also speaks fluent Mandarin Chinese and Russian. These skills have helped him train and consult with scientists from other countries, and to communicate with cosmonauts on the ISS. Chiao has several advanced science degrees, and is a trained pilot. After his career with NASA, Chiao became an author and engineering consultant.

CHAPTER 75
MICHAEL COLLINS

MICHAEL COLLINS (1930–2021) was the command module pilot of NASA's Apollo 11 mission. On July 20, 1969, as fellow astronauts Neil Armstrong and Buzz Aldrin descended to the Moon, Collins stayed behind and flew the orbiting command module *Columbia*.

Collins was born in Rome, Italy. His father was a US Army officer stationed overseas. The family lived in many places, but eventually moved to Washington, DC. After graduating from the United States Military Academy at West Point, Collins joined the US Air Force. He trained to become a fighter pilot. Later, he became a highly skilled test pilot.

Collins joined NASA in 1963. On July 18, 1966, he was launched into orbit aboard the Gemini 10 spacecraft. Collins was the pilot. He flew with astronaut John Young, who commanded the mission. They docked with an unmanned Agena spacecraft. These rendezvous skills would later be needed for Apollo Moon missions. During the three-day mission, Collins performed two extravehicular activities (EVA), which made him NASA's third spacewalking astronaut. In total, he logged over 266 hours in space.

CHAPTER 76
PETE CONRAD

Charles "Pete" Conrad Jr. (1930–1999) flew into space four times. Most people remember him today as the commander of Apollo 12. On November 19, 1969, Conrad and Alan Bean became the third and fourth astronauts to land on the surface of the Moon.

Conrad was born in Philadelphia, Pennsylvania. He was very smart, but school was hard for him because he had dyslexia, a reading disability. He found new ways of learning and eventually earned a degree in aeronautical engineering.

Conrad started flying airplanes when he was a teenager. He joined the US Navy in 1953 and became a fighter pilot. Later, he became a test pilot, which drew the interest of NASA. He was chosen to be an astronaut in 1962.

In addition to his Apollo 12 flight, Conrad flew two Gemini missions and commanded the Skylab 2 space station mission.

CHAPTER 77
GORDON COOPER

LEROY GORDON "GORDO" COOPER JR. (1927–2004) was one of NASA's original Mercury 7 astronauts. In 1963, he commanded a Mercury spacecraft that he named *Faith 7*. Launched into space on May 15, 1963, it was the last and longest Mercury mission. Cooper flew in space for 34 hours while orbiting the Earth 22 times. He also became the first American astronaut to sleep in space.

Cooper was born and grew up in Shawnee, Oklahoma. He became a US Air Force fighter pilot, and then a test pilot. He was selected to become a Mercury astronaut in 1959, the youngest of the group. During his historic flight, he logged more time than all the previous Mercury missions combined.

In 1965, Cooper traveled to space again, this time with astronaut Charles "Pete" Conrad in Gemini 5. Cooper was the commander of the eight-day mission. They circled the Earth 120 times, proving that humans could survive a long trip to the Moon. Cooper became the first person to make two separate orbital flights around the Earth.

CHAPTER 78
YURI GAGARIN

On April 12, 1961, from the Baikonur Cosmodrome in Kazakhstan, a powerful rocket roared to life, launching 27-year-old cosmonaut Yuri Gagarin (1934–1968) into the history books. The moment he lifted off, Gagarin excitedly said, "Poyekhali!" ("Let's go!") That day, he became the first human to travel in space. As the sole crew member aboard the Soviet Union's Vostok 1 spacecraft, Gagarin was also the first person to orbit the Earth.

Yuri Gagarin was born in a small farming village in western Russia. In the 1950s, he learned to fly jets in the Soviet Air Forces. Gagarin was smart, well prepared, and had excellent reactions during emergencies. In 1960, he was chosen to be part of the first group of 20 pilots to train for the Soviet space program.

Gagarin's historic flight lasted 108 minutes and completed one orbit around the Earth. After the mission, he received the title "Hero of the Soviet Union," which was the nation's highest honor. Gagarin never flew in space again, dying tragically in a plane crash in 1968.

CHAPTER 79
JOHN GLENN

IN 1962, JOHN GLENN (1921–2016) became the first American astronaut to orbit the Earth. He flew his *Friendship 7* spacecraft three times around the planet. Glenn was a member of the Mercury 7, the first astronauts chosen by NASA. After his astronaut career, he served as a United States senator, representing the state of Ohio from 1974 to 1999. In 1998, while still a senator, he was a crew member on the space shuttle *Discovery*. At age 77, he was the oldest person to ever fly in space.

John Herschel Glenn Jr. was born in Cambridge, Ohio, on July 18, 1921. He flew in an airplane at age eight with his father. That sparked a lifelong love of flying. In 1942, as World War II raged, Glenn put his college education on hold to enlist for military duty. He became a pilot for the United States Marine Corps, flying dozens of combat missions during World War II, the Chinese Civil War, and the Korean War. He earned the Distinguished Flying Cross medal for heroism six times.

In 1954, Glenn became a test pilot, making sure new plane designs were safe to fly. His experience flying military combat jets served him well. After setting aviation speed and distance records, he drew the attention of NASA. The agency chose him to become an astronaut in 1959 after intense testing and training.

Glenn became a national hero after his historic Mercury mission. He was elected to the United States Senate in 1974, representing his home state of Ohio. He was a firm supporter of NASA, nuclear weapons control, and public service. Glenn continued his support of space exploration after retiring from politics in 1999. In 2012, he received the Presidential Medal of Freedom from President Barack Obama. John Glenn died in 2016 at the age of 95.

CHAPTER 80
GUS GRISSOM

GUS GRISSOM (1926–1967) WAS THE SECOND American astronaut to fly in space. He flew in a Mercury spacecraft he named *Liberty Bell 7*. Like Alan Shepard before him, Grissom's 15-minute flight was suborbital, which means it did not circle the Earth. Boosted into space by a powerful Redstone rocket, Grissom's spacecraft reached a height of nearly 103 miles (166 km).

Virgil Ivan "Gus" Grissom was born and grew up in Mitchell, Indiana. He joined the US Air Force and flew 100 combat missions during the Korean War. He then became a test pilot and engineer.

In 1959, Grissom was chosen by NASA to join its first group of astronauts. They were called the Mercury 7. Grissom went through rigorous training to prepare for his *Liberty Bell 7* flight.

Grissom was the commander of Gemini 3, along with astronaut John Young. The three-orbit flight, on March 23, 1965, made Grissom the first NASA astronaut to fly in space twice.

Gus Grissom was tragically killed in a launchpad fire on February 21, 1967, during a test of the Apollo 1 Moon mission spacecraft. Also killed were fellow astronauts Edward White and Roger Chaffee.

CHAPTER 81
CHRIS HADFIELD

Canadian astronaut Chris Hadfield (b. 1959) flew on two space shuttle missions and later served as commander of the International Space Station (ISS) from March to May 2013. He is the first Canadian to walk in space.

Hadfield was born in Sarnia, Ontario, and grew up on a farm in the southern part of the province. He learned to fly glider aircraft at age 15. After joining the Canadian Armed Forces, he earned a mechanical engineering degree and learned to fly combat fighter jets. He later became a test pilot before joining the Canadian Space Agency, where he trained to become an astronaut.

One of Hadfield's goals is to educate the public about the importance of space exploration. He famously released a music video in 2013 of himself playing guitar in the ISS and singing David Bowie's "Space Oddity." The video has been seen by tens of millions of people on YouTube and other social media outlets.

CHAPTER 82
SCOTT KELLY

SCOTT KELLY (B. 1964) FLEW INTO space four times during his 20-year astronaut career. He is best known for his nearly yearlong stay aboard the International Space Station (ISS). He and Russian cosmonaut Mikhail Korniyenko were chosen to test the effects of long periods of weightlessness on the human body. In addition to his spaceflight experience, Kelly was chosen because he had a twin brother, Mark (who was also an astronaut). Mark remained on Earth. Each had their eyesight, blood, urine, and other body systems checked for differences. The tests were done to find out if humans could live in space for long periods of time. This information may help with future missions to faraway planets, such as Mars.

Kelly was born in Orange, New Jersey. He learned to fly jets in the US Navy and became a test pilot. During his NASA career, he flew the space shuttle twice, and also commanded the ISS. He spent a total of 520 days in space, including 18 hours of spacewalking.

CHAPTER 83
ALEXEY LEONOV

Cosmonaut Alexey Leonov (1934–2019), of the Soviet Union, was the first person to leave his spacecraft on an EVA (extravehicular activity). On March 18, 1965, he left the safety of his capsule and floated in the weightlessness of space. Leonov's spacewalk lasted 12 minutes.

The Voskhod 2 mission was a success, but it almost cost Leonov his life. His spacesuit overinflated, and he could not get back inside his spacecraft to rejoin his crewmate, cosmonaut Pavel Belyayev. Thinking quickly, Leonov released air from his suit and was able to squeeze through the hatch before losing consciousness.

Like cosmonaut Yuri Gagarin, Leonov was a military pilot and part of the first group chosen by the Soviet Union to travel in space. After the Voskhod 2 mission, he commanded his country's half of the Apollo-Soyuz Test Project in 1975 with the United States. Besides his piloting skills, Leonov was a published artist.

CHAPTER 84
JIM LOVELL

JAMES "JIM" LOVELL (B. 1928) TRAVeled to space four times during his NASA career, including trips to the Moon twice. He is best remembered as the commander of the ill-fated Apollo 13, which suffered an explosion on board during the trip to the Moon. Thanks to the ingenuity and calm determination of Lovell and crewmates John Swigert and Fred Haise, plus NASA personnel back on Earth, they returned safely on April 17, 1970, after a nail-biting six-day voyage.

Lovell was born in Cleveland, Ohio, but spent much of his childhood in Milwaukee, Wisconsin. He graduated from the United States Naval Academy in 1948, and then trained to become a US Navy jet pilot. A few years later, he became a test pilot, graduating at the top of his class. He tested new aircraft to make sure the designs were safe for other pilots to fly. In 1962, he applied and was accepted by NASA to become an astronaut.

Lovell's first spaceflight was as the pilot of Gemini 7, along with astronaut Frank Borman. Launched on December 4, 1965, they orbited Earth 206 times over a period of 14 days. The following year Lovell commanded Gemini 12, flying with Buzz Aldrin.

In December 1968, Lovell flew with Frank Borman and William Anders on Apollo 8. Lovell was the command module pilot. It was a risky first voyage to the Moon and back. No human had ever seen the far side of the Moon before. Apollo 8 proved that such a trip was possible.

CHAPTER 85
SALLY RIDE

Astronaut Sally Ride (1951-2012) was born and raised in Los Angeles, California. She joined NASA in 1978, beating out thousands of applicants for the chance to become an astronaut. Five years later, on June 18, 1983, she rode the space shuttle *Challenger* into orbit around the Earth, becoming the first American woman to travel into space. She was a mission specialist who helped deploy communications satellites and conduct scientific experiments. She flew on *Challenger* again in 1984. Ride logged a total of more than 14 days in space during her career.

Despite her history-making flight as the first female astronaut, Ride was proud to simply call herself an astronaut and let her accomplishments speak for themselves. After her NASA career, Ride worked as an author and teacher.

CHAPTER 86
WALLY SCHIRRA

Walter "Wally" Schirra (1923–2007) was chosen in 1959 to become part of the elite Mercury 7, the first group of NASA astronauts. He was the only astronaut to fly Mercury, Gemini, and Apollo space missions.

Schirra was born in Hackensack, New Jersey. He studied engineering in school. He learned to fly jets while serving in the military. During the Korean War, he flew 90 combat missions. He later became a US Navy test pilot.

As a Mercury astronaut, Schirra became the fifth American to fly in space. On October 3, 1962, his *Sigma 7* spacecraft rocketed into orbit. He flew six times around the Earth before safely splashing down in the Pacific Ocean.

In 1965, Schirra flew on Gemini 6A along with astronaut Tom Stafford. They successfully docked with another Gemini spacecraft. Three years later, Schirra commanded the first manned Apollo flight, Apollo 7, along with Donn Eisele and R. Walter Cunningham. The 11-day mission proved Apollo was ready to travel to the Moon.

CHAPTER 87
DAVID SCOTT

DAVID SCOTT (B. 1932) FLEW IN SPACE THREE times. He was the commander of Apollo 15. The mission also included astronauts Alfred Worden and James Irwin. Scott became the seventh person to walk on the Moon. He and Irwin were also the first astronauts to drive on the Moon's surface in a lunar rover.

Scott was born in San Antonio, Texas. He excelled in school and was a star athlete. After a career in the US Air Force flying jet fighters, he joined NASA in 1963. His first spaceflight was with Neil Armstrong aboard Gemini 8 in 1966. He was also the command module pilot for Apollo 9. The 10-day mission included a docking and test flight of the lunar module while in Earth orbit.

CHAPTER 88
ALAN SHEPARD

ALAN B. SHEPARD JR. (1923–1998) WAS A naval aviator who became the second person—and the first American—to travel into space. He piloted the Mercury *Freedom 7* space capsule. The spacecraft was launched atop a Redstone rocket at Florida's Cape Canaveral on May 5, 1961. Just 10 years later, in 1971, Shepard commanded the Apollo 14 Moon mission. He was the fifth person to walk on the lunar surface, and the first person to hit a golf ball on the Moon. He was also the only one of the original Mercury 7 astronauts to land on the Moon.

Alan Shepard was born on November 18, 1923, in Derry, New Hampshire. While growing up in Derry, he became very interested in flying. He served in the United States Navy during World War II. After the war, Shepard became a Navy test pilot. He flew newly designed aircraft to make sure they were safe for other pilots.

In 1959, Shepard became one of NASA's first astronauts. They were a group called the Mercury 7. During Shepard's historic Mercury mission, he flew 116 miles (187 km) high. It was a suborbital mission, which means he did not orbit the Earth. However, he was the first person to control his spacecraft in flight (Yuri Gagarin's flight a month earlier was controlled remotely). Shepard's flight lasted about 15 minutes.

After his Apollo 14 mission in 1971, Shepard became the chief of NASA's Astronaut Office. He served briefly at the United Nations and was promoted to rear admiral of the US Navy. In 1974, Shepard retired from NASA and the Navy, but he continued to support space exploration until his death in 1998.

CHAPTER 89
DEKE SLAYTON

Donald "Deke" Slayton (1924–1993) was one of NASA's original Mercury 7 astronauts. Unfortunately, he was grounded because doctors detected an irregular heartbeat. Instead of flying on a Mercury mission, Slayton became the head of NASA's Flight Crew Operations. He was responsible for crew training, and for choosing which astronauts to send on Gemini and Apollo missions.

Slayton was born and grew up near Sparta, Wisconsin. He flew combat missions during World War II before becoming a test pilot for the US Air Force.

In 1972, Slayton was cleared by doctors to fly once again. Three years later, he finally went into space as part of the Apollo-Soyuz Test Project, which included docking with a Soviet spacecraft. At the time, Slayton was the oldest person to fly in space, at age 51.

CHAPTER 90
VELENTINA TERESHKOVA

Cosmonaut Valentina Tereshkova (b. 1937) became the first woman to fly in space on June 16, 1963. She piloted the Soviet Union's Vostok 6 spacecraft and orbited the Earth 48 times, and is the only woman in history to fly solo in space.

Tereshkova was born in a village in central Russia. She became an expert skydiver, which led to her selection as a cosmonaut. She was chosen from a group of more than 400 applicants to join the Soviet's female cosmonaut corps. She went through intensive training, which included learning to fly jets. She was just 26 years old when she was launched into space.

After her historic three-day spaceflight, Tereshkova rose to the rank of colonel in the Soviet air force. Later, she became active in politics. She also earned a doctorate in aeronautical engineering.

CHAPTER 91
GHERMAN TITOV

GHERMAN TITOV (1935–2000) WAS the second Soviet cosmonaut sent into space. On August 6, 1961, he flew solo aboard the Vostok 2 spacecraft. He was 25 years old, which makes him the youngest person ever to fly in space. He was the first person to circle the globe multiple times, completing 17 orbits around the Earth. During his 25-hour flight, he became the first person to sleep in space. He also was the first to take over manual control of his spacecraft. Even though Titov was a former Soviet air force pilot, he suffered from space sickness, a common kind of motion sickness. That resulted in him holding another record: the first person to vomit in space.

CHAPTER 92
ED WHITE

EDWARD "ED" WHITE (1930–1967) WAS THE first American astronaut to leave his spacecraft and "walk" in space. His extravehicular activity (EVA) on the Gemini 4 mission in 1965 was so much fun he didn't want it to end.

White was born and grew up in San Antonio, Texas. He was a bright student and talented athlete. After first becoming a test pilot for the US Air Force in 1959, he later joined NASA in 1962.

After the success of Gemini 4, White was chosen to be part of the crew of Apollo 1. Tragically, he and fellow astronauts Gus Grissom and Roger Chaffee died in a launchpad fire on January 27, 1967.

CHAPTER 93
PEGGY WHITSON

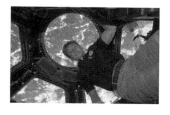

PEGGY WHITSON (B. 1960) WAS THE first female commander of the International Space Station (ISS). She is NASA's most experienced astronaut, with over 665 days in space. She has spacewalked 10 times, for a total of more than 60 hours. That gives her the record for most extravehicular activities (EVAs) by a woman. She was 57 years old during her last mission to the ISS in 2017, which made her the oldest woman astronaut in space.

Whitson was born in Mount Ayr, Iowa, and grew up on a farm near Beaconsfield. She earned a doctorate in biochemistry from Rice University, and began working for NASA in 1989 as a biochemist. A dedicated scientist and explorer, she started astronaut training in 1996.

Beginning with her first trip to the ISS in 2002 as a science officer, Whitson made a total of three long-duration missions to the space station. She was the commander of the ISS twice, in 2007-2008, and in 2017. She was also the chief of NASA's Astronaut

Office from 2009 to 2012. Whitson retired from NASA in June 2018. She later joined private space company Axiom Space, and will be a mission commander for an upcoming commercial flight to the ISS early in 2023.

CHAPTER 94
JOHN YOUNG

JOHN YOUNG (1930–2018) WAS THE longest-serving astronaut in NASA's history. His experience and steady personality earned him legendary respect among other astronauts. He went into space six times during his 42-year career. His missions spanned three major space programs: Gemini, Apollo, and the space shuttle. He walked on the Moon, and commanded the very first space shuttle into orbit. As the chief of NASA's Astronaut Office for 13 years, Young was a tireless supporter of spaceflight training and safety.

John Watts Young was born in San Francisco, California, on September 24, 1930. He spent most of his childhood in Orlando, Florida. He earned a degree in aeronautical engineering in 1952 from the Georgia Institute of Technology. Young soon joined the Navy and served during the Korean War. After the war, he became a Navy test pilot. He broke speed and altitude records testing F-4 Phantom II military jets.

In 1962, Young was chosen by NASA to become an astronaut. He trained for many months to prepare for the complexity and dangers of spaceflight. The one-man Mercury program was coming to an end, so Young trained for the two-man Gemini missions.

In 1965, Young flew in Gemini 3—the first manned Gemini mission—along with astronaut Gus Grissom. He used his test pilot skills to evaluate the new spacecraft. The mischievous Young also smuggled aboard a corned beef sandwich, which he shared with Grissom. The following year, Young commanded Gemini 10, accompanied by astronaut Michael Collins. They practiced docking with other spacecraft. It was a skill astronauts would later need during the Apollo Moon missions.

In May 1969, Young piloted the command module of Apollo 10. He became the first person to fly solo around the Moon. Crewmates Thomas Stafford and Eugene Cernan departed in the lunar module to practice flying a few miles above the Moon. Young stayed behind and controlled the command module alone. When Stafford and Cernan returned, Young used the docking skills he learned in the Gemini program to join the command module with the lunar module. It was the first time two spacecraft docked together while orbiting the Moon. The practice mission was a success, paving the way for the historic Apollo 11 Moon-landing mission in July 1969.

In 1972, Young returned to the Moon. He commanded the Apollo 16 mission, which also included crewmates Charles Duke and Ken Mattingly. This time, Young descended to the lunar surface, together with Duke. The pair spent over 20 hours walking and driving on the Moon. They collected rock samples and performed many science experiments.

Young served as the chief of NASA's Astronaut Office from 1974 to 1987. He oversaw crew assignments. He also helped test and evaluate NASA's new space shuttle program. In 1981, he commanded the first orbital flight of the *Columbia* spacecraft. In

1983, he again commanded *Columbia* on a 10-day, science-heavy mission with a crew of five other astronauts.

After the space shuttle *Challenger* disaster in 1986, Young worked tirelessly to improve astronaut safety on space shuttles and the International Space Station.

By his retirement in 2004, Young had worked for 42 years for NASA. He flew more than 835 hours in space, but his contributions to the American space program are too great to be measured. John Young died in 2018 at the age of 87.

ALSO IN THE DESTINATION OUTER SPACE SERIES

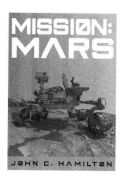

Join award-winning science writer John Hamilton as he investigates Mars, describing its hold on humankind's imagination and exploring the latest scientific efforts to unveil its secrets.

Mission: Mars tells the story of the Red Planet, from ancient folklore to modern orbiters and rovers surveying its dusty surface. Every mission is covered, from the Mariner orbiters to the Viking landers, from the Curiosity rover to future Mars colonies. Vital information about the planet includes its geology, atmosphere, gravity, and orbit. Also covered are geographical wonders such as Valles Marineris (the Grand Canyon of Mars) and Olympus Mons (the largest volcano in the solar system), as well as major craters, icy poles, and Mars's two moons, Phobos and Deimos.

Why is Mars named for the Roman god of war? Did people really think Earth was being invaded by Martians during Orson Welles' *War of the Worlds* radio broadcast of 1938? What is the truth behind the mysterious "Face of Cydonia" on the surface of Mars? These questions and more are answered in these inspiring

—and sometimes humorous—stories of myth, science, and exploration.

Perfect for school reports, but also a thrilling book for anyone interested in space, young or old.

In this 34,000-word exploration of Mars, you'll discover:

• The impact of Mars on modern culture, including H.G. Wells' classic *The War of the Worlds*, Ray Bradbury's masterpiece *The Martian Chronicles*, and modern works such as Andy Weir's *The Martian*.

• The promise and challenge of terraforming Mars.

• The fleet of orbiters sending jaw-dropping images of the Red Planet's surface.

• More than 100 breathtaking images from NASA's archives.

• Diagrams and detailed maps.

• The search for water and microbial life.

• NASA's Orion and Space Launch System, which may one day take humans to Mars.

• Glossary and Timeline.

• Aligned to Common Core Standards and correlated to state standards.

• And much, much more!

Mission: Mars is thoroughly researched and easy to read. Own your own copy to discover the allure, tragedies, and triumphs of the mysterious Red Planet!

Click here for more information on Amazon Kindle: Mission: Mars

Or scan the QR code below with your smart device:

GET A FREE BOOK

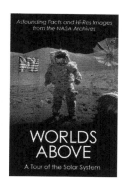

If you enjoyed this book, join my readers' group and get a free copy of *Worlds Above*, an exploration of the solar system. My newsletter is how I keep my loyal readers up-to-date about my latest releases, and send news about my writing and research trips. Click below to get started.

Get my free book

Or scan the QR code below with your smart device:

PLEASE LEAVE A REVIEW

If you enjoyed *The Space Race,* please consider leaving a review. Reviews are the lifeblood of independent authors. They help new readers who might be on the fence. They also help me discover what's working and what could use improvement. I do so enjoy hearing from my readers. It would mean a lot to me if you would add a line or two, or even simply add a star rating. Thanks, and happy reading!

Go directly to the Amazon review page by clicking the following link:

The Space Race

Or scan the QR code below with your smart device:

TIMELINE

The Space Race

1926—American scientist Robert Goddard becomes the first person to build and test a rocket using liquid fuel.

1939, September 1—World War II begins with Germany's invasion of Poland.

1942—German scientist Wernher von Braun builds and launches the first V-2 missile for Nazi Germany's war effort. Over the next three years, thousands of V-2s will be built by slave laborers from concentration camps.

1945—Wernher von Braun surrenders to American soldiers. World War II ends. Dr. von Braun and about 125 of his associates go to Fort Bliss, Texas, to build missiles for the United States.

1950—Wernher von Braun and his team go to the Redstone Arsenal near Huntsville, Alabama. They will design the US Army's Redstone and Jupiter ballistic missiles, as well as the Jupiter C, Juno II, and Saturn I launch vehicles.

1955—President Dwight Eisenhower announces that the United States will attempt to launch the world's first artificial satellite to orbit the Earth during the upcoming International Geophysical Year in 1957-58. Soon after Eisenhower's announcement, Premier Nikita Khrushchev announces that the Soviet Union will also attempt to launch a satellite.

1957, August 21—The first successful flight of the Soviet R-7 Semyorka, the world's first intercontinental ballistic missile (ICBM).

1957, October 4—The Soviet Union launches the Sputnik 1 satellite. It marks the unofficial start of the space race.

1957, November 3—The Soviet Union launches Sputnik 2 into orbit. It contains various scientific instruments, plus a dog named Laika.

1957, December 6—American Vanguard rocket explodes on the launchpad. It is a great embarrassment to the United States.

1958, January 31—The United States launches Explorer 1, the first American satellite in space.

1958, October 1—NASA (National Aeronautics and Space Administration), a US government agency, officially begins work. Its original primary objective is to create Saturn rockets to fly to the Moon. Today it is a civilian agency, separate from the military, that coordinates and carries out America's space activities, both manned and unmanned.

1958, November 28—The United States makes its first successful launch of an Atlas intercontinental ballistic missile (ICBM).

1959, April 9—NASA announces the names of the first seven astronauts chosen for the American space program. The "Mercury 7" included Alan Shepard, Gus Grissom, Gordon Cooper, Wally Schirra, Deke Slayton, John Glenn, and Scott Carpenter.

1960—Wernher Von Braun becomes director of NASA's Marshall Space Flight Center and the chief architect of the Saturn V launch vehicle.

1960, August—The first successful launch of a Corona reconnaissance satellite.

1961, January 31—Ham becomes the first chimpanzee in space. Ham returns safely, but technical problems cause NASA to delay sending a human into space.

TIMELINE

1961, April 12—Cosmonaut Yuri Gagarin becomes the first human in space. He completes one orbit of the Earth in his Soviet Vostok 1 spacecraft and returns safely to Earth.

1961, May 5—Astronaut Alan Shepard becomes the first American in space. Shepard pilots his *Freedom 7* spacecraft in the 15-minute Mercury-Redstone 3 mission, which is watched on TV by millions.

1961, May 25—President John F. Kennedy gives a speech to Congress explaining his vision of America's role in space exploration. He challenges NASA to land a man on the Moon "before the decade is out."

1961, July 21—Astronaut Virgil "Gus" Grissom becomes the second American in space aboard his *Liberty Bell 7* capsule. His mission is marred by an unexplained blowing of his hatch door after splashdown.

1961, August 6—Cosmonaut Gherman Titov blasts off in his Vostok 2 spacecraft. Only 25 years old, he will stay in orbit for more than 24 hours.

1962, February 20—Astronaut John Glenn travels to space aboard his *Friendship 7* capsule. He becomes the first American to orbit Earth.

1962, May 24—Astronaut Scott Carpenter orbits the world three times in his *Aurora 7* capsule. He photographs the Earth and performs many experiments during the Mercury-Atlas 7 mission.

1962, August 11 & 12—The Soviet Union launches Vostok 3 and 4 within a day of each other. Each capsule carries a cosmonaut who will stay in orbit around the Earth for several days.

1962, October 3—Astronaut Walter "Wally" Schirra performs a 6-orbit flight in his *Sigma 7* capsule. The Mercury-Atlas 8 mission lasts more than 9 hours.

1963, May 15-16—Astronaut Gordon "Gordo" Cooper blasts off in his *Faith 7* spacecraft, the final Mercury mission. He spends 34 hours, 19 minutes, 49 seconds in space, completing 22 orbits of the Earth to evaluate the effects of one day in space on a human.

1963, June 14 & 16—The Soviet Union launches Vostok 5 and

6. The capsules orbit the Earth, flying within three miles (5 km) of each other to see how difficult it might be to rendezvous two spacecraft. Valentina Tereshkova becomes the first woman in space as the cosmonaut aboard Vostok 6.

1964, April 8—Gemini 1 goes up in an unmanned test flight. Data is collected for three of its 63 Earth orbits before its reentry destruction.

1964, October 12—The Soviet Union launches Voskhod 1 with three cosmonauts aboard, the most occupants of any spacecraft so far.

1965, January 19—Unmanned Gemini 2 tests its heat shield.

1965, March 18—Cosmonaut Alexey Leonov becomes the first person to spacewalk when he floats free of his Voskhod 2 capsule.

1965, March 23—Gemini 3 astronauts Gus Grissom and John Young test systems and equipment in the first manned Gemini mission.

1965, June 3-7—Gemini 4 astronauts James McDivitt and Ed White spend more than four days orbiting the Earth, NASA's first multiday mission. Astronaut White becomes the first American to spacewalk.

1965, August 21-29—Gemini 5 astronauts Gordo Cooper and Pete Conrad spend eight days in orbit, breaking the endurance record.

1965, October 25—Gemini 6 mission is scrubbed after the unmanned Agena Target Docking Vehicle explodes shortly after launch.

1965, December 4-18—Gemini 7 astronauts Frank Borman and Jim Lovell spend 14 days in space. Gemini 6A astronauts Wally Schirra and Tom Stafford rendezvous with them on December 15. The two spacecraft fly next to each other for more than four hours.

1966, March 16—Gemini 8 astronauts Neil Armstrong and David Scott meet up with an orbiting Agena and successfully dock with it. The astronauts nearly meet with tragedy when a thruster malfunctions sending their capsule spinning, but they land safely on Earth.

1966, June 3-6—Gemini 9A astronauts Tom Stafford and Gene Cernan face several mishaps, including being unable to dock with the unmanned Agena and serious spacewalking issues for Cernan.

1966, July 18-21—Gemini 10 astronauts John Young and Michael Collins dock with two Agena spacecraft. Collins performs two EVAs.

1966, September 12-15—Gemini 11 astronauts Pete Conrad and Richard Gordon fly their capsule higher than any other manned spacecraft has ever flown. Gordon has trouble with his spacewalk.

1966, November 11-15—Gemini 12 astronauts Jim Lovell and Buzz Aldrin conduct experiments. Aldrin devises ways to work outside the capsule, and spends a successful five and a half hours spacewalking.

1967, January 27—Apollo 1 astronauts Gus Grissom, Ed White, and Roger Chaffee are killed in a fire in the capsule while training. Their deaths will result in new safety standards for future manned missions.

1967, April 23—First launch of a Soyuz spacecraft with a crew.

1967-1968—Unmanned test flights of Apollo 4, 5, and 6 (there was no Apollo 2 or 3).

1968, October 11-22—Apollo 7 astronauts Wally Schirra, Walt Cunningham, and Donn Eisele fly the first manned mission since the Apollo 1 tragedy. They test the command and service modules.

1968, December 21-27—Apollo 8 astronauts Frank Borman, Jim Lovell, and William Anders orbit the Moon and take the first "Earthrise" photo.

1969, March 3-13—Apollo 9 astronauts James McDivitt, David Scott, and Russell Schweickart test the lunar module while orbiting Earth.

1969, May 18-26—Apollo 10 astronauts Tom Stafford, John Young, and Gene Cernan travel to the Moon and descend partway in the lunar module.

1969, July 16-24—Apollo 11 astronauts Neil Armstrong, Buzz Aldrin, and Michael Collins travel to the Moon. On July 20, Armstrong and Aldrin descend to the lunar surface. When Armstrong became the first human to step on the Moon, he uttered these famous words: "That's one small step for a man, one giant leap for mankind."

1969, November 14-24—Apollo 12 astronauts Pete Conrad, Richard Gordon, and Alan Bean travel to the Moon. Conrad and Bean descend to the lunar surface. They collect rocks and conduct experiments.

1970, April 11-17—Apollo 13 astronauts Jim Lovell, Jack Swigert, and Fred Haise, two days into their mission, survive an explosion that cripples their spacecraft and puts them in extreme danger. The world waits breathlessly until the astronauts return safely to Earth.

1971, Jan. 31-Feb. 9—Apollo 14 astronauts Alan Shepard, Stuart Roosa, and Edgar Mitchell travel to the Moon. Shepard and Mitchell go down to the surface for EVAs. Shepard hits two golf balls.

1971, April 19—The Soviet Union's Salyut 1 space station is launched into orbit. It is the world's first space station.

1971, July 26-Aug. 7—Apollo 15 astronauts David Scott, James Irwin, and Al Worden travel to the Moon. First lunar roving vehicle is driven.

1971, July 29—The crew of Soyuz 11 reenters Earth's atmosphere after a successful three-week mission aboard the Salyut space station. Tragically, a faulty valve on the spacecraft opens and causes the crew cabin to depressurize. All three Soviet cosmonauts are killed.

1971, October 11—Salyut 1 deorbits and burns up in Earth's atmosphere.

1972, April 16-27—Apollo 16 astronauts John Young, Ken Mattingly, and Charles Duke travel to the Moon. Young gives the rover a speed test.

1972, December 7-19—Apollo 17 astronauts Gene Cernan,

Harrison Schmitt, and Ronald Evans travel to the Moon. They conduct experiments and collect samples. Gene Cernan becomes the last man to walk on the Moon. Their mission ends Project Apollo.

1973, May 14—America's first space station, Skylab, is launched into orbit around Earth.

1975, July 15—The Apollo-Soyuz Test Project is launched, a joint mission between the United States and the Soviet Union. Spacecraft from each country meet on July 17 and stay docked for two days.

1979, July—Skylab deorbits and burns up in Earth's atmosphere.

1981, April 12—Space shuttle *Columbia* launches, the first orbital flight of an American space shuttle.

1986, January 28—Space shuttle *Challenger* explodes shortly after launch, killing all seven astronauts aboard.

1986, February 20—First module of the Soviet Union's Mir space station goes into orbit.

1991, December 25—The Soviet Union collapses. Part of the country becomes the Russian Federation, commonly known today simply as Russia. The Mir space station comes under the control of Russia.

1994–1995—Soviet cosmonaut Valery Polyakov sets a space endurance record of 438 consecutive days aboard the Mir space station.

1998, November 20—The first piece of the International Space Station, the Russian module Zarya, is launched into orbit.

1998, December 6—The first American module of the International Space Station, Unity, is attached to the Soviet module Zarya. First connection between two modules of the space station.

2001, March 23—Mir space station is deorbited. It burns up and disintegrates over the Pacific Ocean.

2003, February 1—Space shuttle *Columbia* disintegrates shortly before landing, killing all seven astronauts aboard.

2006, July 12—American company Bigelow Aerospace launches Genesis 1 unmanned experimental space habitat.

2011, July 8—Space shuttle *Atlantis* launches, the last flight of an American space shuttle.

2011, September 29—Chinese Tiangong-1 space station is launched.

2020s—NASA's Lunar Orbital Platform Gateway plans to launch and enter cislunar space between Earth and the Moon.

GLOSSARY

Astronaut
Someone who travels in a spacecraft. The word has Greek roots that stand for "star sailor," or "star traveller."

Canadarm
The Canadarm and Canadarm2 robotic arm systems were developed and made in Canada. Canadarm was used on the space shuttle. Canadarm2 is currently used on the International Space Station (ISS) to help assemble and repair ISS modules. It can also capture and dock unmanned supply spacecraft.

Cold War
The Cold War was a time of political, economic, and cultural tension between the United States and its allies and the Soviet Union and other Communist nations. It lasted from about 1947, just after the end of World War II, until the early 1990s, when the Soviet Union collapsed and Communism was no longer a major threat to the United States.

Cosmonaut
An astronaut from Russia or the former Soviet Union.

Cupola

A dome-shaped module on the ISS. It is attached to the larger Tranquility module. It was built in Italy and attached to the ISS in 2010. Its large windows give astronauts a panoramic view of the Earth. The circular central window is 31.5 inches (80 cm) in diameter, the largest window ever used in space.

Diameter

The distance through the center of an object, from one side to the other.

Dock

When either two spacecraft or a spacecraft and a space station are joined together.

Extravehicular Activity (EVA)

An EVA is any activity for which astronauts must go outside the protected environment in which they live while in space. A spacewalk is an EVA.

G-Force

Pressure on a human body caused by the force of gravity or from fast acceleration. Astronauts and pilots experience strong G-forces during takeoffs, making them feel many times heavier than their normal body weight.

Gyroscope

A mechanical device often used in aircraft and spacecraft that provides stability and aids in navigation.

International Space Station (ISS)

An Earth-orbiting space station designed by NASA, the European Space Agency, the Russian Federal Space Agency, the Japan Aerospace Exploration Agency, and the Canadian Space Agency, as well as other countries around the world. The ISS allows astronauts and scientists to live and work in space. Construction of the ISS began in orbit in 1998.

National Aeronautics and Space Administration (NASA)

A United States government space agency started in 1958. Its original primary objective was to create Saturn rockets to fly to the Moon. NASA's goals today include space exploration and increasing people's understanding of Earth, our solar system, and the universe. It is a civilian agency, separate from the military.

Orbit

The circular path a moon or spacecraft makes when traveling around a planet or other large celestial body.

Payload

Something that is carried by an aircraft, rocket, or missile. Rockets can carry bombs, satellites, or spacecraft containing human astronauts or cosmonauts.

Sea of Tranquility

Apollo 11's Neil Armstrong and Buzz Aldrin landed in the Sea of Tranquility. It is a large region of the Moon made mostly of basalt rock. Early astronomers once thought the dark areas of the Moon were filled with water. That is why they are named for seas. In reality, they are dark because the rocks are rich in iron, which reflects less light.

Soviet Union

A former country that included a union of Russia and several other Communist republics. It was formed in 1922 and existed until 1991.

Space Shuttle

American's first reusable space vehicle. NASA built five orbiters: *Columbia, Challenger, Atlantis, Discovery,* and *Endeavour.*

Two shuttles and their crews were destroyed by accidents: *Challenger* in 1986, and *Columbia* in 2003.

Space Sickness

A type of motion sickness that affects some astronauts in space. Symptoms include an upset stomach, dizziness, and vomiting.

Splashdown

When Mercury, Gemini, and Apollo spacecraft returned to Earth, they landed in the ocean—thus, a splashdown.

Stage

In order to fly as high as possible, some rockets have more than one section, called stages. Each stage has its own engine and fuel. They are stacked on top of each other. When the first stage runs out of fuel, it drops away and falls toward Earth.

Test Pilot

A person who flies new or experimental aircraft to test the machine's flight worthiness and to make sure it is safe for other pilots to fly.

Trapezoid

A four-sided shape where the top is slightly smaller than the bottom. The *Liberty Bell 7* spacecraft first used this shaped window, allowing astronaut Gus Grissom a better view from space.

Van Allen Belts

Zones of radioactive charged particles, shaped like huge donuts, that encircle the Earth. Most of the particles come from the solar wind and are captured by Earth's magnetic field. They are named for Dr. James Van Allen, a space scientist who worked at the University of Iowa. His instruments aboard the Explorer 1 and 3 satellites first proved the existence of the radiation belts.

WARHEAD

Usually an explosive, a warhead is a kind of bomb that is sent to its target by a missile or rocket. Instead of explosives, some warheads carry toxic chemicals or harmful germs.

SELECTED BIBLIOGRAPHY

- "A Brief History of NASA." NASA History Division | NASA, 25 July 2005, www.history.nasa.gov/factsheet.htm.
- "About Marshall." NASA, 13 Feb. 2015, www.nasa.gov/centers/marshall/overview/about.html.
- "About Project Mercury." NASA, 6 Apr. 2015, www.nasa.gov/mission_pages/mercury/missions/program-toc.html.
- "Animals in Space." NASA History Division | NASA, 3 Apr. 2014, history.nasa.gov/animals.html.
- "Apollo 11 (AS-506)." National Air and Space Museum, airandspace.si.edu/explore-and-learn/topics/apollo/apollo-program/landing-missions/apollo11.cfm.
- "Artemis Program." NASA, 4 June 2019, www.nasa.gov/artemisprogram.
- "At what altitude does weightlessness occur in outer space?" YouTube, www.youtube.com/watch?v=FWvurbWerCA.
- "Before 'one Small Step': How Apollo 8 Became Our First True Moon Shot." NBC News, 17 Dec. 2018,

SELECTED BIBLIOGRAPHY

www.nbcnews.com/mach/science/one-small-step-how-apollo-8-became-our-first-true-ncna945961.
- Blue Origin, www.blueorigin.com.
- Chaikin, Andrew. A Man on the Moon: The Voyages of the Apollo Astronauts. Penguin, 2007.
- "Ep 71: Apollo and The Moon." NASA, www.nasa.gov/johnson/HWHAP/apollo-and-the-moon.
- European Space Agency, www.esa.int.
- "EVA-3 Close-out." www.hq.nasa.gov/alsj/a17/a17.clsout3.html.
- "1st American in Orbit: How John Glenn (And NASA) Made History (Infographic)." Space.com, 8 Dec. 2016, www.space.com/14618-nasa-john-glenn-orbit-friendship-7-50th-anniversary.html.
- "Gateway." NASA, 5 Dec. 2019, www.nasa.gov/gateway.
- "Gemini 3." Encyclopedia Astronautica, www.astronautix.com/g/gemini3.html.
- "Gemini 4." Encyclopedia Astronautica, www.astronautix.com/g/gemini4.html.
- "History - The Flight of Apollo-Soyuz." NASA History Division | NASA, history.nasa.gov/apollo/apsoyhist.html.
- Hollingham, Richard. "V2: The Nazi Rocket That Launched the Space Age." BBCpage, www.bbc.com/future/article/20140905-the-nazis-space-age-rocket.
- "How NASA's Gemini Spacecraft Worked (Infographic)." Space.com, 3 June 2015, www.space.com/29549-how-nasa-gemini-spacecraft-worked-infographic.html.
- "International Space Station." NASA, 12 Jan. 2015, www.nasa.gov/mission_pages/station/main/index.html.

SELECTED BIBLIOGRAPHY

- "July 20, 1969: One Giant Leap For Mankind." NASA, 19 Feb. 2015, www.nasa.gov/mission_pages/apollo/apollo11.html.
- Kranz, Gene. *Failure Is Not an Option: Mission Control From Mercury to Apollo 13 and Beyond.* Simon & Schuster, 2009.
- "The Launch of Vostok Spacecraft." RussianSpaceWeb.com, www.russianspaceweb.com/vostok1_launch.html.
- "'Man, I Gotta Pee': 55 Years Since Freedom 7 Began America's Adventure in Space (Part 1)." AmericaSpace, 30 Apr. 2016, www.americaspace.com/2016/04/30/man-i-gotta-pee-55-years-since-freedom-7-began-americas-adventure-in-space-part-1/.
- "Moon in Google Earth - Apollo 11 Landing." YouTube, www.youtube.com/watch?v=6R3j1NU2nQM.
- "The Most Extreme Human Spaceflight Records." Space.com, 23 Apr. 2019, www.space.com/11337-human-spaceflight-records-50th-anniversary.html.
- "NASA Former Astronauts." NASA, 8 Jan. 2016, www.nasa.gov/astronauts/biographies/former.
- "NASA History Media Resources." NASA, www.nasa.gov/content/nasa-history-media-resources.
- "NASA Schedules First Manned Gemini Flight From Cape Kenney." NASA, www.nasa.gov/sites/default/files/atoms/files/gemini_iii_presskit.pdf.
- NASA. *Saturn V Flight Manual.* WWW.Snowballpublishing.com, 2012.
- NASA, NASA.gov.
- "The Partnership: A History of the Apollo-Soyuz Test Project." NASA History Division | NASA, history.nasa.gov/SP-4209/cover.htm.
- "Photos of Rockets and Missiles." Historic Spacecraft - Photos of Rockets and Spacecraft, historicspacecraft.com/rockets.html.

- "Preparations for EVA-1." www.hq.nasa.gov/alsj/a12/a12.eva1prep.html.
- "Press Kits." NASA History Division | NASA, history.nasa.gov/alsj/alsj-prskits.html.
- "Project Apollo: Astronaut Biographies." NASA History Division | NASA, history.nasa.gov/ap11ann/astrobios.htm.
- "Project Mercury." NASA History Division | NASA, history.nasa.gov/SP-4001/cover.htm.
- "Results of the Second U.S. Manned Suborbital Space Flight July 21, 1961." NASA History Division | NASA, history.nasa.gov/MR-4/chap04.htm.
- "Rocket and Missile System." Encyclopedia Britannica, www.britannica.com/technology/rocket-and-missile-system.
- "Rocket Propulsion | How Things Fly." Homepage for How Things Fly, howthingsfly.si.edu/propulsion/rocket-propulsion.
- Shepard, Alan, and Deke Slayton. Moon Shot: The Inside Story of America's Race to the Moon. Turner Pub, 1995.
- "The Space Race (1955-1975)." YouTube, www.youtube.com/watch?v=xvaEvCNZymo.
- "Space Race | National Curriculum | Schools & Colleges | National Cold War Exhibition." National Cold War Exhibition, www.nationalcoldwarexhibition.org/schools-colleges/national-curriculum/space-race/.
- SpaceX, www.spacex.com.
- "Tsiolkovsky solves the problem of traveling to space, with ROCKET (how rocket work)." YouTube, www.youtube.com/watch?v=lOiEKqTCHsQ.
- "The TV cameras Apollo left on the Moon." YouTube, www.youtube.com/watch?v=hPOjkSYv3lA.

- "Two Become One: How the Apollo Spacecraft Stuck Together." Popular Science, 26 Apr. 2021, www.popsci.com/two-become-one-how-apollo-spacecraft-stuck-together/#page-2.
- "U-2 Incident (1960)." YouTube, www.youtube.com/watch?v=RZZdpNV75iA&list=PLu2xst_eS6doPJgFLMveVh-Yngjb8rVFbs&index=10.
- "V-2 Anatomy." National Air and Space Museum, airandspace.si.edu/exhibitions/space-race/online/sec200/sec211.htm.
- "Valentina Tereshkova: First Woman in Space." Space.com, 22 Jan. 2018, www.space.com/21571-valentina-tereshkova.html.
- "Vladimir Komarov and the Tragic Flight of Soyuz 1." www.spacesafetymagazine.com/space-disasters/soyuz-1/tragic-death-vladimir-komarov/.
- "What Was Apollo 11's Reentry Speed at Parachute Deployment?" Space Exploration Stack Exchange, space.stackexchange.com/questions/2661/what-was-apollo-11s-reentry-speed-at-parachute-deployment.
- "Who Are The Most Famous Astronauts?" Universe Today, www.universetoday.com/45089/famous-astronauts/.
- "Why Are Astronauts Weightless?" YouTube, www.youtube.com/watch?v=iQOHRKKNNLQ.
- Wood, Brenden M. The Space Race: How the Cold War Put Humans on the Moon. Nomad Press, 2018.

ABOUT THE AUTHOR

John C. Hamilton has spent most of his life in Minnesota. His first job was in the news media—delivering papers. He has worked as a house painter, a delivery driver, a corn shucker in a factory, and a movie usher learning the art of cinema, and life, in a darkened theater.

With a degree in photojournalism and mass communication in hand, he launched a career in magazine editing, which led to writing and editing books. After 40 years in the trenches, he is now a bestselling author of more than 300 nonfiction books for young adults, plus three novels and 13 screenplays, several of which have been optioned by Hollywood studios.

John's young adult book *Battle of the Little Bighorn* earned 2015 Spur Award Finalist honors from the Western Writers of America. He is a two-time winner of the Golden Duck Award for Excellence in Children's Science Fiction Literature, and his epic retelling of the Lewis & Clark expedition, *Lewis & Clark: Adventures West*, was a Minnesota Book Award finalist for Young Adult Nonfiction. *School Library Journal* said "(Hamilton's) books present a remarkable amount of information and provide readers with a clear understanding of complicated issues."

John can be found most summers with his family either exploring the American West or hiking along Minnesota's rugged North Shore.

Connect with John at:
www.johnchamilton.com
john@johnchamilton.com

Scan the QR code below with your smart device to go to John's website at www.johnchamilton.com:

ALSO BY JOHN C. HAMILTON

For the latest books and news, scan the QR code below with your smart device:

Heroes and Villains of the Wild West

Wild Bill Hickok

Wild Bill Hickok was a man of many skills: pioneer of the Great Plains, Civil War scout and spy, lawman, gambler, stagecoach driver, showman. When he drew his weapon, it was with one aim: to kill. Wild Bill is brought to life in this easy-to-read title by award-winning Western author John Hamilton. *Wild Bill Hickok* is part of the bestselling Heroes and Villains of the Wild West hardcover series, now available for the first time as an ebook! Perfect for school reports, but a gripping tale for anyone captivated by the Wild West.

Jesse James

Jesse James was a villain to most people, a hero to others. He was a Missouri farmer, a ruthless Confederate guerrilla fighter, a loving husband and father, and a robber of banks, trains, and stagecoaches. He led a gang of desperadoes on a 16-year crime spree that sprawled over at least eight states. Jesse James is brought to life in this easy-to-read title by award-winning Western author John Hamilton. *Jesse James* is part of the bestselling Heroes and Villains of the Wild West hardcover series, now available for the first time as an ebook! Perfect for school reports, but a gripping tale for anyone captivated by the Wild West.

Other Nonfiction

Lewis & Clark: Adventures West

Originally published in hardcover and a Finalist at the 17th Annual Minnesota Book Awards, now available for the first time as an ebook! Perfect for school reports, but a gripping tale for everyone, young or old. Featuring 187 images; 4 maps; travel tips; glossary; index. *"An excellent stepping stone to in-depth adult titles such as Stephen E. Ambrose's Undaunted Courage."* — School Library Journal

Fiction

Ghost Marshal

All hell breaks loose when a badass woman meets a gunslinging ghost.

Jessie Parker is a woman on a mission: to avenge her father's brutal murder. But in 1876 Deadwood, she has about as much chance as a wax cat in hell—until she partners with the cantankerous ghost of Wild Bill Hickok. They soon find themselves knee-deep in gunfights, Chinese sorcery, barroom brawls, pleasures of the flesh, demon owls, forbidden romance, and a heaping dose of frontier justice. Along the way, Jessie and Bill uncover a bizarre conspiracy that takes them near enough to hell to smell smoke.

Isle Royale

Shipwrecks, gangsters, and the mother of all storms. Living in a lighthouse can be murder. How far would you go to be a hero?

Isle Royale is an adventure story filled with plot twists and compelling characters. If you like fast-paced excitement, danger on the high seas, and tales of bravery and redemption, then you'll love John Hamilton's page-turning thriller.

Printed in Poland
by Amazon Fulfillment
Poland Sp. z o.o., Wrocław